Unraveling the Service Parts Supply Chain

Understanding Complexity, Confronting Challenges, Driving Change

Mark Brenzikofer

Table of Contents

ACKNOWLEDGMENTS

I first want to acknowledge my family for their support and patience throughout the long journey and time commitment involved in writing my first book. Thank you for your patience.

I would also like to send a special thank you to Dr. Roger Kerin, Professor of Marketing at SMU's Cox School of Business (Retired), for his steadfast guidance, encouragement, and literary enlightenment on book structure and layout.

Thank you as well to Dr. Rahul Singh, Founder of ThinkQ AI, for his guidance, brainstorming sessions, and domain expertise in Service Parts Supply Chain Management.

I want to express my gratitude to Jay Abramson, Principal, at J Lewis Solutions, for reviewing the manuscript and providing thoughtful suggestions and feedback.

With regards to the book publication, I would like to recognize Larry Butler for his copy-editing skills and publishing support and acknowledge Ahmed Zaeem for the book cover design.

Introduction

The term "supply chain" is widely recognized. Every company that produces goods relies on a supply chain. The COVID-19 pandemic brought massive disruptions to global supply chains, with issues such as supply shortages, transportation challenges, and customer hoarding making headlines. "Supply chain" is a broad term encompassing the sourcing of raw materials, manufacturing, distribution, return, and **MRO (Maintenance, Repair, and Operations)** for any product sold today. While this process is quite linear, it faces significant challenges in practice—as seen during the pandemic, when a breakdown at any step disrupted the entire flow.

The **Service Parts Supply Chain (SPSC)**, however, is different from the traditional supply chain, commonly called the forward supply chain. Many executives classify SPSC under the MRO process or group it with Logistics and Distribution. On the surface, the SPSC's process steps and path to the customer may resemble those of the forward supply chain. The terminology is familiar, and practitioner training often shares roots with traditional supply chain disciplines. But dig deeper, and you'll discover that the SPSC operates under a far more complex business model.

Having worked with numerous Fortune 500 and Fortune 100 companies over the past thirty years within service parts supply chains, I've seen firsthand how little those outside the SPSC understand its complexity. Many fail to grasp how decisions made by other business units inadvertently contribute to that complexity. To senior executives, SPSC often appears as disorganized chaos. For those within SPSC, it feels more like semi-organized chaos. During quarterly business reviews, executives often face underperforming metrics, escalating inventory levels, and lagging customer satisfaction scores.

Unspoken questions often arise:

- "Why is this so difficult?"

- "Do we need all this complexity—why not simply stock the necessary parts?"

- "Why don't we face these challenges in the forward supply chain?"

- "Why keep spending money on improvements if performance never seems to improve?"

This book is designed primarily for executives and managers who want to better understand SPSC without getting lost in technical details. It also serves as a valuable introduction for those new to the field, providing insights into what to expect and the challenges ahead. For seasoned SPSC professionals, this book offers new perspectives on the complexities you navigate every day, along with practical takeaways to enhance your strategy and execution.

The first half of the book focuses on comparing the similarities and differences between the forward and service parts supply chains. From there, we will dive deeper into the key challenges SPSC organization need to navigate.

The latter half of the book introduces practical approaches and solutions to move toward an improved understanding of the structure and nuances of the SPSCM.

Every service parts supply chain has unique complexities, even though some fundamentals are shared. This book does not aim to cover every technical edge case—but it offers a clear, experience-driven perspective on a field that remains underexplored yet critically important.

Chapter 1

Call to Action:
Confronting the Realities of
Service Parts Supply Chain Management

The **Service Parts Supply Chain (SPSC)** is often overlooked—overshadowed by the forward supply chain. Yet, it is in SPSC where complexity truly reigns. It operates in an environment of uncertainty, low-volume demand, stringent **service level agreements (SLAs)**, and an overwhelming variety of difficult problems to solve—factors that render traditional supply chain strategies ineffective.

Every grounded aircraft, failed medical device, or stalled industrial machine represents more than just operational downtime—it signals a potential hit to brand reputation, strained customer relationships, and significant financial consequences. The ability to respond with speed, accuracy, and cost-efficiency, delivering the right part at the right time, is no longer a logistical goal—it's a strategic imperative.

Despite its critical importance, SPSC remains underrepresented in supply chain literature. Many organizations continue to retrofit forward supply chain practices into service environments—with disappointing results. The cost of misalignment is high: delayed repairs, SLA violations, dissatisfied customers, and eroded brand equity. This book challenges that outdated approach. It highlights the unique characteristics of SPSC and offers practical frameworks based on real-world experience.

Whether you're a supply chain leader, a field service strategist, or a systems architect, you are part of an ecosystem that cannot afford to treat service parts as an afterthought. The message is clear: it's time to challenge conventional assumptions, abandon linear thinking, and adopt an adaptive, multidimensional approach to service operations.

To better understand the dynamics of SPSC, we must shift our lens from linear logistics to system-based thinking. The book introduces the **Five-Forces of SPSCM Operations**—a foundational framework encompassing **Business Demands, Data, Technology, People,** and **Processes**. These are not abstract concepts; they are operational forces that shape how service supply chains function under pressure:

- **Business Demands** define what must be delivered, at what speed, and under which constraints.

- **Data** serves as the foundation—capturing, predicting, and enabling smarter decisions.

- **Technology** enables execution—automating workflows, optimizing allocation, and increasing visibility.

- **People** add the human element—making judgment calls, resolving exceptions, and driving continuous improvement.

- **Processes** are the outcomes—defining how service is delivered, measured, and refined.

These forces operate as an interconnected system. Understanding their interdependencies is essential—not just for solving problems, but also for designing supply chains that can scale, adapt, and thrive.

This book is a practical guide through that complexity. It provides an important foundation for those who know that service parts cannot be managed with yesterday's playbook and are ready to rethink the assumptions limiting supply chain performance today.

Breaking Down Supply Chain Models: Why Service Parts Are Different

Traditional supply chains—common in retail, manufacturing, and consumer goods—are built around **predictability, volume efficiency**, and **repeatability**. They rely on stable demand signals, long production runs, and tightly synchronized logistics to minimize costs and maximize throughput. Success in these environments is often measured by how well the system standardizes processes, reduces lead times, and avoids inventory waste through tools like just-in-time (JIT) replenishment and lean operations.

In contrast, service parts supply chains are built around **uncertainty, responsiveness**, and **availability**. Instead of stable demand, they face sporadic, low-volume requests driven by unpredictable failures and urgent repair needs. Success depends not on minimizing inventory, but on strategically positioning the right parts—often slow-moving—across a decentralized network to meet tight service windows. Flexibility, visibility, and risk mitigation replace efficiency as the dominant priorities.

While supply chains may follow models like make-to-stock, make-to-order, and configure-to-order, service parts rarely conform to a single approach. They often operate within a hybrid system, blending demand-driven strategies with condition-based triggers. Managing returns, planning repairs, and orchestrating reverse logistics requires a fundamentally different mindset—one that assumes uncertainty is the rule, not the exception.

SPSC must combine capabilities: the responsiveness of a demand-driven model, the flexibility of custom configurations, and the foresight of predictive analytics. These systems must operate across field service, depot repair, inventory control, logistics, and support—despite constraints like part scarcity, long lead times, and ever-evolving configurations.

What distinguishes SPSC is not just what moves through it, but how it must move—adaptively, responsively, and often in real time. It's a system of continuous recalibration, where complexity is the norm and reliability is the goal.

Use Case: Aerospace Aircraft on Ground Urgency

In aerospace, SPSC is mission critical. Airlines operate under rigorous maintenance schedules and strict regulatory oversight. When an aircraft is grounded due to a missing part—known as an AOG (Aircraft on Ground) event—the cost can reach $150,000 per day in lost revenue, rerouting, and passenger compensation.

The complexity is staggering. There are thousands of components with varying maintenance cycles, lifespans, and failure probabilities. Some are rarely needed yet must be globally available at a moment's notice. Others are highly regulated, require refurbishment, or must be serialized and certified before reuse. Sourcing, transporting, and tracking these parts often spans international borders and complex reverse logistics.

Traditional supply chain approaches, based on historical demand and forecast models, fall short. In AOG scenarios, these events demand real-time, condition-based planning. Airlines now integrate sensor data, usage history, weather patterns, and maintenance logs to proactively anticipate part failures.

To meet these needs, aerospace leaders use distributed inventory hubs, predictive analytics, and dynamic allocation engines. Many partner with specialized 3PLs (third-party logistics providers) for critical part positioning and just-in-time delivery. This orchestration—balancing cost, risk, and responsiveness—is a perfect example of the specialized thinking required in SPSCM.

Here, logistics becomes resilience. The service parts supply chain protects not just uptime, but passenger safety and brand credibility. That's why aerospace service parts strategies are being emulated across other industries where service failure is simply not an option.

Use Case:
Medical Device Field Service and Uptime Management

In healthcare, the stakes are even higher. Medical devices—MRI machines, ventilators, surgical robots—are essential to patient care. A single malfunction can delay diagnoses, halt treatment, or jeopardize lives. In this context, delayed service is not just inconvenient—it's unacceptable.

Imagine an MRI machine that breaks down midweek. It may support dozens of scans per day. When it goes offline, hospitals must cancel appointments, reroute patients, and absorb the cost of lost productivity. The service supply chain must respond swiftly—with the correct part, a qualified technician, and delivery often within hours.

The challenge? Many of these parts are high-cost, low-frequency items not stocked on-site. The OEM (Original Equipment Manufacturer) or service partner must quickly determine:

- What part is needed?
- Where is it located?
- Can it meet the SLA?
- Is a technician available?

Service operations here rely on distributed **field stocking locations (FSLs)**, predictive maintenance alerts, and tight integration across call centers, dispatch systems, and parts depots. Regulatory oversight adds another layer, requiring traceability, repair histories, and use of approved components.

In this model, the key metric is not cost per unit—it's uptime and reliability. Leaders in this space prioritize analytics, proactive part positioning, and emergency delivery options, including couriers and mobile stock units strategically located near hospitals for rapid deployment.

This is SPSC in its most critical form—high stakes, low margin for error, and zero tolerance for delay. Behind every part is a mission that must not fail.

Common Features of Forward and Service Parts Supply Chains

The **Forward Supply Chains (FSC)** and SPSC share several core features that underpin their effectiveness. At the heart of both lies procurement and purchasing—each relies on source materials and components from external suppliers to meet production or service needs. Accurate demand forecasting is also a critical shared function, as both supply chains depend on anticipating future requirements to optimize stock levels and avoid shortages or overstocking.

Shared Features

	Forward Supply Chain	Service Parts Supply Chain
Purchase Material from External Suppliers	✓	✓
Forecast Future Demand	✓	✓
Demand Model Drives Operations – Push/Pull	✓	✓
Store and Maintain Inventory	✓	✓
Maintain a Distribution Network	✓	✓
Logistic & Transportation Routing	✓	✓
Customer Service Focused	✓	✓

Additionally, both supply chains operate on a combination of demand models: customer-driven "pull" strategies for immediate needs and forward-looking "push" models based on forecast and strategic planning. Inventory management is another common thread; whether stocking finished goods in FSC or spare parts in SPSC, maintaining the right inventory balance is essential to meeting service levels. Both systems also rely on robust distribution networks that include warehouses and distribution centers to position inventory closer to the end user. Effective logistics planning ensures that transportation routes, carrier selection, and delivery schedules align with customer expectations. Finally, customer service plays a vital role in both models, supporting inquiries, resolving delivery issues, and ensuring a positive customer experience across the supply chain lifecycle.

Key Differences of Forward and Service Parts Supply Chains

While the FSC and the SPSC share foundational elements such as procurement, planning, and distribution, their goals, architecture, and execution models differ greatly. FSCs are built around centralized, high-efficiency systems that emphasize volume, consistency, and unit cost reduction. SPSC, by contrast, is inherently decentralized and designed to deliver agility—focused on rapid response, asset uptime, and compliance with service-level commitments. It must react quickly to urgent, often unpredictable needs across dispersed geographies, where even brief delays can cause serious financial or operational impact.

These distinctions are amplified by the different timelines they support. The FSC completes its role once a product is manufactured and shipped, typically ending at the point of sale or delivery. The SPSC, however, begins where the FSC ends—extending across the entire post-sale lifecycle, which may span years or decades. This long-tail responsibility introduces added complexity, requiring ongoing support for aging equipment and legacy parts through multiple generations of use.

The contrast also plays out in how demand is generated and anticipated. FSC demand tends to follow forecasted patterns based on orders or market trends, making it relatively steady and easier to plan. In the SPSC, demand is failure-driven—sporadic, low-frequency, and difficult to predict using conventional models. As a result, inventory strategies differ. FSC operations aim for turnover and efficiency, whereas SPSC inventories must be distributed, diverse, and ready—not optimized for velocity, but for availability. The goal is not just to move product efficiently, but to ensure the right part is in place when and where it's needed most.

Forward Supply Chain versus Service Parts Supply Chain

		Forward Supply Chain	Service Parts Supply Chain
01	Purpose, Direction and Responsiveness	Operates in a linear, centralized model focused on scale and cost control.	Operates in a dynamic, decentralized model prioritizing speed, uptime, and service level commitments.
02	Lifecycles	Lifecycle ends when the product stops production.	Lifecycle continues until the product reaches the end of usable life—often years or decades later.
03	Point of Supply	Focuses on delivering a finite number of new products.	Manages the flow of individual parts to support many revisions of operational products post-sales.
04	Demand Source Comparisons	Demand is tied to sales forecasts and customer orders, making it more predictable.	Demand arises when a part fails, making it highly unpredictable and difficult to forecast.
05	Inventory Management	Inventory is optimized for high-volume, fast-moving products using JIT or lean practices.	Stocks a wide range of low-demand, slow-moving parts while balancing high cost and risk of unavailability.

Fundamental Management Challenges in a Service Parts Supply Chain

Service parts supply chain management (SPSCM) presents five fundamental challenges:

1. Diversity of Service Models

Unlike traditional FSCs that typically support standardized product flow, SPSCM must accommodate a wide range of service delivery models. These include in-warranty repairs, extended service contracts, pay-per-incident models, and outsourced technical support through third-party providers. Each model brings its own forecasting, inventory, and logistical requirements—making it difficult to apply uniform planning approaches across the network.

2. Dynamics of Demand Forecasting

Forecasting in SPSCM is complicated by the unpredictable nature of service demand. Failures occur at irregular intervals and are influenced by a range of factors, including product age, usage intensity, and environmental conditions. While historical data provides some guidance, planners must account for sudden shifts in demand due to new product launches, end-of-life cycles, or changes in installed base behavior.

3. The OEM Field and Maintenance Multi-Echelon Network

Original Equipment Manufacturers (OEMs) must support service activity across multiple inventory tiers—central warehouses, regional hubs, country stockrooms, and field technician locations. Coordinating part availability across this multi-echelon network adds significant complexity, especially when response times are dictated by contractual obligations. Ensuring coverage without excessive inventory buildup requires fine-tuning planning and continuous network optimization.

4. Inventory Control

Service parts inventory often has long shelf lives, limited repurposing options, and unpredictable turnover. Overstocking leads to obsolescence and write-offs, while understocking impacts service levels and customer satisfaction. Effective control hinges on managing inflows (including repairable returns), optimizing regional redistribution, and leveraging demand modeling that accounts for preventative maintenance, reactive repairs, and lifecycle stage.

5. Impact of Product Entitlements

Product entitlements—such as warranties, SLAs, and uptime guarantees—determine the service obligations tied to each asset in the field. These commitments directly affect how much inventory must be pre-positioned and how quickly parts must be delivered. Variations in entitlement coverage across the installed base require nuanced planning strategies to balance customer expectations with cost-effective service delivery.

Moving Forward

Over the next five chapters, we will explore the **key differences** (mentioned earlier) between the forward supply chain and service parts supply chain highlighted above, including:

1. **Purpose and Direction** – To highlight the distinct purpose of both supply chains—product delivery versus post-sales support—that drive contrasting strategies in structure, responsiveness, and operational priorities
2. **Lifecycles Comparisons** – A detailed look at lifecycle differences
3. **Points of Supply** – A closer examination of supply chain product variations
4. **Demand Source & Predictability** – Understanding how demand forecasting differs
5. **Inventory Management** – Contrasting how inventory supports the operation

In the second section, Chapters 7 through 11, we will break down the five inherent management challenges in a service parts supply chain.

1. **Diversity of Service Models**
2. **Dynamics of SPSC Demand Forecasting**
3. **The OEM Field Repair and Maintenance Multi-Echelon Inventory Network**
4. **Inventory Control**
5. **The Impact of Product Entitlements on the SPSCM**

From this foundation, the third section of the book (starting with Chapter 12) will explore the critical infrastructure and external forces that add to the complexity of an already challenging SPSCM environment. We will discuss:

1. **Data as the Lifeblood of SPSCM: Visibility, Accuracy, and Operational Efficiency**
2. **Technology as the Backbone of SPSCM: Aligning Systems for Performance**
3. **Shared Ownership: How Cross-Functional Alignment Drives SPSCM Success**
4. **Mergers, Acquisitions, and the Fragmentation Risk in SPSCM**

Finally, in the fourth section of the book, we'll introduce the Five-Forces of SPSCM model, and explore how each force shapes every decision within the SPSCM operation. The focus will be on:

1. **Defining the Five-Forces of SPSCM Operations** and explore the relationships among the forces
2. **Examining the dynamics of each of these forces** in greater detail and how their relationship defines the DNA, unique to each SPSCM operation
3. Discussing an approach on how to **uncover any underlying inefficiencies in the Five-Forces through a comprehensive assessment**

Part 1

Forward Supply Chains and Service Parts Supply Chains: A Comparison

Chapter 2

Difference #1:
Purpose, Direction, and Responsiveness

Introduction Summary

Modern supply chains are not a one-size-fits-all operation. Companies must operate multiple supply chain models tailored to the unique demand of different products, market segments, and customer needs. At the heart of the differentiation lies a core distinction between **Forward Supply Chain Management (FSCM)** and **Service Parts Supply Chain Management (SPSCM)**. FSCM focuses on efficiently producing and delivering finished goods to customers, optimizing for scale, cost, and throughput. SPSCM, in contrast, exists to support the ongoing service, repair, and maintenance of products after the initial sale—where responsiveness, availability, and speed are paramount.

These two models serve fundamentally different business purposes. While FSCM operates linearly and predictably—from raw materials to finished goods—SPSCM is dynamic, decentralized, and shaped by the uncertainty of part failures and service needs. As this chapter explores, the operational logic, planning approaches, and strategic objectives of FSCM and SPSCM diverge in significant ways. Recognizing these differences is critical for organizations aiming to excel not only at delivering products but also at sustaining long-term customer satisfaction and equipment performance. The ability to align supply chain design with the purpose and direction of each model ultimately determines a company's ability to compete and thrive across the full lifecycle of its products.

The Domains of Forward and Service Parts Supply Chains

Simply stated, a **Forward Supply Chain (FSC)** is the end-to-end network of organizations, people, information, and physical resources involved in designing, producing, and delivering a product to a customer. It encompasses everything from raw material procurement to manufacturing, warehousing, transportation, distribution, and retail. This network functions as the backbone of how businesses convert inputs into market-ready goods and get them into the hands of consumers or business buyers. The FSC culminates at the point of sale, where ownership is transferred to the customer. Figure 2-1 illustrates a typical forward supply chain structure that demonstrates this linear demand-driven journey.

Figure 2-1

Typical Forward Supply Chain Structure

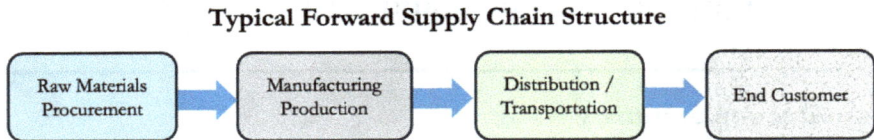

The FSC is typically designed for scale, efficiency, and cost control. Its configuration is often centralized, with clearly delineated stages where each function aims to maximize output and minimize unit cost. This model excels in environments defined by consistency and forecastable demand—conditions that support lean workflows, extended production cycles, and consolidated fulfillment. High-volume processing, bulk procurement, and optimized scheduling all contribute to minimizing surplus inventory, reducing waste, and increasing throughput. Practices like Lean Manufacturing, Six Sigma, and Just-in-Time (JIT) are particularly effective in forward chains, reinforcing principles of quality, precision, and continuous operational refinement.

The administration of a forward supply chain is referred to as **Forward Supply Chain Management (FSCM)**—the structured process of planning, coordinating, and optimizing the flow of goods, data, and finances along the forward path of the supply chain. FSCM is foundational to every FSC as it is the structured approach to managing this process with goals centered around efficient market coverage, competitive pricing, and service-level consistency.

In contrast, a **Service Parts Supply Chain (SPSC)**—sometimes referred to as the aftermarket supply chain—is a distinct, often parallel network that supports the repair, maintenance, and servicing of products already in use. The SPSC ensures that spare parts, repair components, and associated resources are available post-sale to extend product lifespans, support uptime, and meet maintenance obligations. Whether the part is a medical scanner component, a turbine blade, a circuit board, or a laptop battery, the SPSC's mission is clear: have the right part in the right place at the right time to minimize disruption. Figure 2-2 provides a visual overview of a typical service parts supply chain.

Figure 2-2

Typical Service Parts Supply Chain Structure

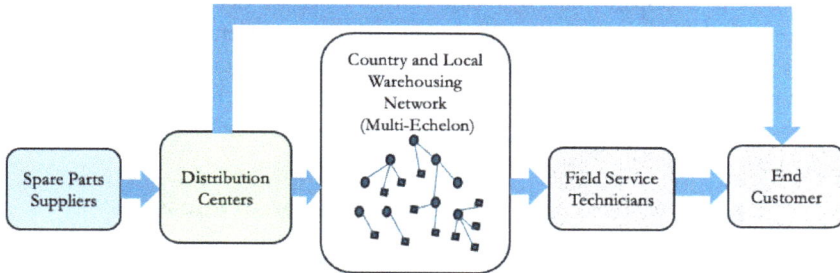

Service Parts Supply Chain Management (SPSCM) is the discipline of overseeing this network to ensure reliability, responsiveness, and cost-effective service delivery. It is the process of initiating, integrating, coordinating, and overseeing the availability and timely access to spare parts for scheduled maintenance, and to minimize equipment downtime. SPSCM is critical in industries where product uptime is paramount and service expectations are high, such as aerospace, healthcare, telecommunications, capital equipment, and information technology (IT) infrastructure. In these industries, a single component failure can mean safety risk, regulatory non-compliance, production downtime, or lost revenue—making responsiveness not just a competitive advantage, but a contractual necessity.

Unlike FSCMs that prioritize throughput and efficiency, SPSCM operations are optimized for **urgency and unpredictability**. They must be nimble enough to respond to sporadic, failure-driven demand patterns. When a high-value machine fails unexpectedly, speed becomes more important than cost, and service organizations must react swiftly to reduce downtime and meet SLAs. While a delayed retail product might inconvenience a customer, a delayed turbine repair can ground an aircraft or halt an entire production line—leading to reputational damage and financial loss.

This service-driven focus requires a completely different operational posture. Where FSCM centralizes inventory for economies of scale, SPSCM must often decentralize stock into regional or even hyperlocal field stocking locations. These nodes may carry expensive, slow-moving parts purely as insurance against failure. In such environments, **redundancy is not waste—it's a requirement.** Its primary objective is not to move volume efficiently, but to respond rapidly to sporadic, unpredictable needs, and to minimize downtime per incident. When a critical component fails—whether in an aircraft, medical device, or piece of heavy capital equipment—the priority shifts instantly from cost efficiency to speed of recovery. Demand forecasting is more complex, relying not just on historical usage but on predictive models that factor in product age, operating environments, usage patterns, and telemetry data.

Moreover, the decision-making in SPSCM tends to be decentralized and time-sensitive, often involving field technicians, support centers, and automated systems that must work together in real time. Investments in digital tools—such as predictive analytics, AI-driven demand planning, real-time inventory tracking, and service execution platforms—are crucial enablers of success in this space.

Purpose, Direction, and Responsiveness

Attribute	FSCM	SPSCM
Primary Objective	Deliver product efficiently and at scale to end customer	Ensure rapid availability of parts for post-sales service and repair
Flow Direction	Linear: raw materials → production → customer	Multi-directional: inventory → field location ←→returns/repair
Network Structure	Centralized, and consolidated	Decentralized, and distributed (multi-echelon)
Inventory Strategy	Minimize inventory, maximize turnover (JIT)	Maintain buffer stock for readiness and uptime
Decision Focus	Cost efficiency, throughput, and production planning	Responsiveness, service levels, downtime mitigation
Production Model	Batch-oriented, long production runs	No production—focus on stocking, deployment, and reverse logistics
Service Level Goals	Order fulfillment, lead times	SLA adherence, uptime, and failure rate
Forecasting Input	Sales orders, market trends, promotional plans	Historical failure rates, installed base, product lifecycle, and service entitlements
Response Time Expectations	Days to weeks	Minutes to hours (often under 2-4 hours)
Reverse Logistics	Low (mostly end-of-life returns)	High (core returns, repairs, refurbishments, warranty processing)
Inventory Turnover Expectations	High turnover, lower obsolescence risk	Low turnover, high obsolescence risk

Attribute	FSCM	SPSCM
Planning Horizon	Long-term (month to years)	Short-term (days to weeks), real-time adjustments

Ultimately, these two domains—FSCM and SPSCM—serve different strategic roles. The forward supply chain delivers the product and underpins revenue growth, market penetration, while minimizing cost per unit. The service parts supply chain preserves the product's value, sustains customer trust, and often contributes to a company's recurring revenue and brand reputation long after the initial sale. Organizations that attempt to manage their service parts supply chain using forward logistics principles risk underperforming in both areas. Recognizing the distinctive nature of SPSCM—and equipping it with dedicated infrastructure, technologies, and governance—is a key enabler of long-term business resilience and customer satisfaction.

Chapter Supply Use Case: Heavy Equipment Manufacturer – Forward versus Service Parts Supply Chain

Consider a global manufacturer of construction and mining equipment. On the forward supply chain side, the company ships thousands of machines annually, through a centralized manufacturing network. These machines are produced in batches, based on long-term forecasts from global sales regions. The supply chain is optimized for cost efficiency: components are sourced and built in low-cost regions, production runs are scheduled months in advance, and finished goods are shipped via ocean freight to regional distribution hubs. Lead times are long but manageable because customers often place orders months ahead of delivery.

Now contrast this with the company's service parts operation. Once a machine is deployed—often in a remote mining site or urban construction site—it becomes decentralized from the company's centralized manufacturing network. If a hydraulic pump fails on a large excavator mid-operation, the cost of downtime can reach tens of thousands of dollars per hour due to halted work and idle crews. The forward supply chain model, with its long lead times and centralized distribution, is ill-suited to this level of urgency.

To respond, SPSCM operates a network of field stocking locations (FSLs), regional parts depots, and mobile technicians. The supply chain must be agile, responsive, and customer-focused—completely diverging from the batch efficiency logic of the forward operations.

This case highlights a key truth: **while the forward supply chain is built for scale and savings, the service parts supply chain is built for resilience and speed**. Both are critical, but they operate under different rules—and must be managed accordingly.

Chapter 3

Difference #2:
Lifecycles—A Comparison

Chapter Overview

The lifecycle of a product is a crucial factor in strategic planning and forecasting for any business that manufactures a product. **Every product progresses through a lifecycle, from its initial introduction to the market to its inevitable decline and end of life (cradle to grave).**

Understanding where a product stands within the lifecycle is essential for sales initiatives, marketing campaigns, manufacturing, and the Service Parts Supply Chain. Recognizing that a product follows a predictable lifecycle path enables business planners to anticipate both short-term and long-term forecasts. In essence, it serves as a "leading indicator" that can be tracked and analyzed as the product matures.

During this chapter, we will define the product lifecycle curve and discuss its different stages. Then we will compare and contrast its use in the forward and service parts supply chain and how the time horizon is a key differentiator between the two.

The Product Lifecycle Curve: A Foundation for Planning

The **Product Lifecycle Curve (PLC)** is a graphical representation of the planned life of a product in the marketplace. It is a future outlook on how the product will evolve in the market over time. The product curve progresses through distinct stages, from introduction to end of life. Each stage represents a different set of market dynamics, customer expectations, and operational strategies. The product PLC curve is typically bell-shaped, with product volume represented on the vertical axis and time on the horizontal axis.

- A steep curve indicates rapid growth.
- A shallow curve reflects slower progress.
- The duration of each stage varies significantly by product.

For example:

- Mobile phones may complete the cycle within a few years due to rapid technological advancements.
- Capital equipment or heavy machinery may span decades before reaching end-of-life.

Stages of the Product Lifecycle Curve:

- **Introduction:** A product is newly launched, and demand is uncertain. Production is often limited. Supply chains during this phase must be flexible, ready to scale, and able to support rapid learning and feedback loops.
- **Growth**: Demand accelerates as the product gains market acceptance. The supply chain shifts focus to scalability, cost control, and distribution expansion. Inventory turnover improves, and more predictable patterns emerge.
- **Maturity**: Demand starts to materialize. Products are widely adopted, and the market starts to saturate. Efficiency becomes critical as companies compete on cost and service.
- **Sustaining**: The product reaches maximum penetration, with no further growth.
- **Decline**: Demand wanes due to technology shift, changing customer preferences, or product obsolescence.
- **End of Life**: The product is no longer sold or supported by the company.

When launching a new product and planning for lifetime support, organizations rely heavily on the product lifecycle curve (or a variation of it) as a critical tool for planning and forecasting.

Product Lifecycle Curve and Stages

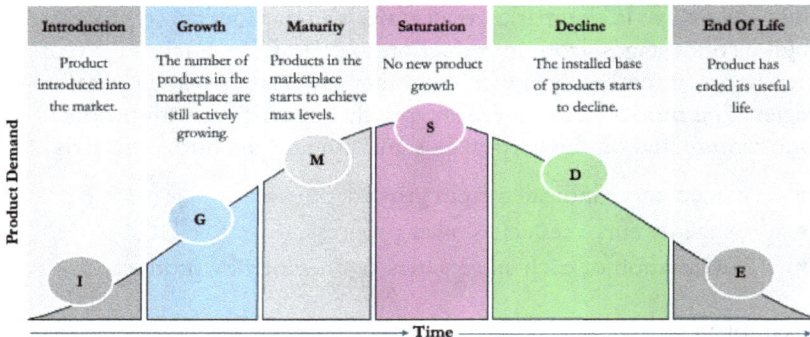

Introduction	Growth	Maturity	Saturation	Decline	End Of Life
Product introduced into the market.	The number of products in the marketplace are still actively growing.	Products in the marketplace starts to achieve max levels.	No new product growth	The installed base of products starts to decline.	Product has ended its useful life.

Forward Supply Chain and its Relationship to the Product Lifecycle Curve

The relationship between the forward supply chain and the product lifecycle curve is tightly bound by the time horizon—that is, the span of time over which a product is actively managed, marketed, and supported. In the forward supply chain, this time horizon aligns closely with the active life of the product, spanning the Introduction, Growth, and Maturity stages of the product lifecycle. Once a product enters Saturation and the Decline stages, forward supply chain activities typically wind down, as focus shifts to newer models and products.

During the early lifecycle stages, the forward supply chain is geared for agility and responsiveness. In the Introduction stage, demand is uncertain and production volumes are low. Supply chain planners must work with flexible suppliers, manage short runs, and often expedite shipments. As the product transitions into the Growth stage, the supply chain evolves into a high-throughput operation—scaling to meet increasing demand, streamlined distribution, and leveraging volume to reduce unit costs.

In the Maturity stage, the forward supply chain reaches peak efficiency. Forecasting becomes more accurate, inventory turnover is high, and standardized processes allow for cost control at scale. However, as the product enters Saturation and the Decline stages, the forward supply chain begins to contract its time horizon. Procurement slows, production is phased out, and resources are reallocated to newer offerings. At this point, the forward supply chain essentially ends its engagement, as the product is no longer the focus of marketing and replenishment strategies.

Forward Supply Chain Lifecycle
(Starts earlier, Ends earlier)

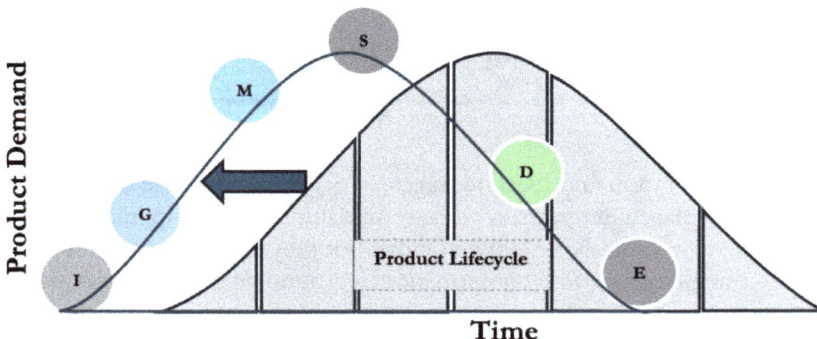

This limited time horizon is what sets the forward supply chain apart from the service parts supply chain, which extends far beyond the typical lifecycle endpoint. While the forward supply chain winds down with the product's commercial viability, the need for spare parts and repair may persist for years or decades—especially in regulated or capital-intensive industries. Therefore, **forward supply chains are time-bound and lifecycle-limited**, optimized for efficiency and volume within a constrained window, while service supply chains must plan for longevity, uncertainty, and support long after the forward supply chain has ceased operations.

Service Parts Supply Chain and its Relationship to the Product Lifecycle Curve

In contrast to the forward supply chain, the service parts supply chain operates across a much longer and less predictable time horizon, extending well beyond the end of a product's commercial life. While the forward supply chain's involvement tapers off during the Saturation stage of the product lifecycle, service parts supply chain management (SPSCM) becomes increasingly important—often taking over as the primary operational focus once the forward logistics wind down. This is particularly true in industries such as aerospace, medical devices, industrial machinery, and defense, where products are expected to remain in service for 10, 20, or even 30+ years.

Service Supply Chain Lifecycle Coverage

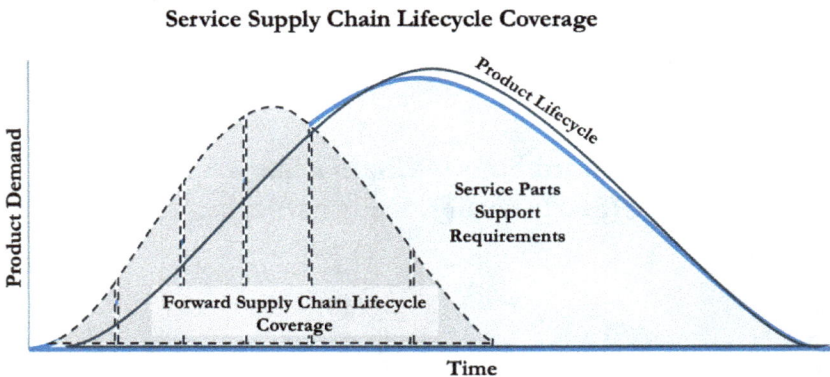

In the Post-Saturation and Decline stages, SPSCM manages the ongoing demand for replacement parts, repairs, refurbishments, and upgrades. These demands may be sporadic and low volume, but they are often mission-critical—a single unavailable component can ground an aircraft, delay patient diagnostics, or shut down a manufacturing line. As such, the **service supply chain must remain highly responsive, flexible, and resilient, even as**

demand becomes more fragmented and the supply base for aging parts begins to shrink.

Moreover, the SPSCM time horizon includes planning for end-of-life (EOL) strategies, last-time-buys, reverse logistics, obsolescence management, and support for legacy systems. While the forward supply chain thrives on standardization and scale, the service parts supply chain must adapt to aging configurations, reduced data visibility, and diminishing supplier engagement. **This longer time horizon requires more nuanced risk management, predictive planning, and often, creative sourcing or engineering solutions to support legacy products**.

Ultimately, while the forward supply chain is designed for the active selling phase of a product, SPSCM is designed for the sustainment and support phase—a timeline measured not in years of commercial activity, but in decades of operational reliability. This fundamental difference in time horizon reinforces why service parts supply chains must be managed as a distinct discipline, with unique capabilities and strategies that extend far beyond the lifecycle limits on the forward supply chain.

Key Takeaways of Lifecycle Differences

The product lifecycle is not a rigid, linear path—it is a dynamic journey influenced by industry practices, technological evolution, customer expectations, and regulatory frameworks. One of the most important takeaways is that lifecycle timing varies significantly across products. A smartphone may move from introduction to obsolescence in under two years, while a locomotive or medical device could remain in use for decades. These differences mean that supply chain strategies must be customized by industry and product type, with both the forward and service supply chains adjusting at different points to meet shifting demands.

Lifecycle overlap across product generations introduces additional complexity. When a new product is released, earlier versions do not simply disappear— they continue to operate in the field, requiring ongoing support. As a result, FSCM focuses on ramping up production and delivery for the latest model, while the SPSCM organization must maintain availability for both old and new generations. This overlap can persist for years and demands precise coordination to ensure adequate part availability without incurring excess inventory costs.

Customer expectations further extend the lifecycle, particularly in industries where uptime, compliance, or safety are critical. Even after a product's commercial availability ends, customers expect reliable support. As products progress from growth to maturity and decline, the focus of the supply chain also shifts—to cost optimization, proactive risk management, and structured end-of-life planning.

A key strategic shift during the decline phase involves obsolescence and last-time-buy planning. Organizations may need to procure and store sufficient quantities of parts that are no longer being manufactured, ensuring they can continue to support products well into the future. These decisions carry significant financial risk and require accurate forecasting, warehousing capacity, and lifecycle planning. Finally, regulatory milestones often add another layer of responsibility—particularly in sectors like healthcare and aerospace—where supply continuity is mandated by law, making lifecycle management a matter of compliance as well as customer service.

Product Lifecycle Coverage Requirements

Attribute	FSCM	SPSCM
Lifecycle Stage Timing is Not Uniform	Adapts pace of production and distribution based on market dynamics	Must adjust to extended support durations, especially in capital goods sectors
Lifecycle Coverage Overlap Across Product Generations	Focus shifts to new generations; old generations phase out quickly	Must support both old and new products for their entire usable lifecycle
Post-Market Support Expectations	Typically ends with last sale; support fades with product retirement	Extended lifecycle responsibilities; must support products for years or decades beyond end-of-sale
Lifecycle-Driven Supply Chain Shifts	Emphasizes rapid scale-up and efficiency in early stages, then cost control and phase-out planning	Evolves from provisioning to precision logistics; must remain agile during decline and after-sales support periods
Obsolescence and Last-Time-Buys	Plans final production runs and clears inventory at product end-of-life	Makes strategic "last-time-buys" to support future service needs; involves high-risk, long-term inventory commitment

Attribute	FSCM	SPSCM
Regulatory and Compliance Milestones	Generally focused on production standards during active sales period	Must maintain traceability; certified components, and compliance documentation for years post-production

Chapter Summary Use Case: Commercial Aircraft Manufacturer

Company Background

A global aerospace company designs and manufactures commercial aircraft. Its operations include managing both the production and delivery of new aircraft (FSCM) and supporting those aircraft with service parts and maintenance over several decades (SPSCM).

Scenario Overview

FSCM – Aligned with Product Launch and Sales Lifecycle

When a new aircraft model is developed, the forward supply chain is configured to:

- Ramp up during production introduction
- Peak during full-rate production
- Gradually taper off as the model nears obsolescence

This lifecycle typically spans ten to fifteen years, during which:

- Demand is highly correlated to sales contracts
- Production volumes are forecastable
- Suppliers are coordinated to align with build schedules
- Logistics are optimized for batch shipments and cost efficiency

Once production ends, FSCM winds down. Suppliers transition to other models or industries, and production lines are retooled.

SPSCM – Extended Lifecycle for Post-Sales Support

However, the aircraft themselves remain in service for 25-30+ years. This necessitates a long tail of aftermarket support for replacement parts, maintenance kits, and system upgrades—long after the FSCM has stopped producing the aircraft.

The SPSCM must:

- Forecast demand based on part failure rates, not sales
- Maintain inventories for components that may not be manufactured anymore
- Coordinate last time buys and obsolescence planning
- Ensure availability for parts that are safety-critical or regulated

As aircraft age, the demand profile shifts from proactive support (scheduled maintenance) to reactive support (unplanned failures), and from OEM-provided parts to potentially third-party or refurbished options.

Lifecycle Divergence in Action

At year 20 post-launch:

- FSCM has completely exited the picture—production facilities are now manufacturing newer models.
- SPSCM is still actively supporting hundreds of aircraft in service worldwide, managing a complex global network of inventory and repair capabilities.

This lifecycle divergence creates a need for separate strategies, systems, and KPIs between FSCM and SPSCM, even though they support the same physical product.

Chapter 4

Difference #3:
Point of Supply – Types of Products

The forward supply chain management (FSCM) and service parts supply chain management (SPSCM) may both handle the same physical product at different points in its lifecycle, but the nature of what the product represents—and how it must be supported—varies significantly. In the forward supply chain, the product is typically new, standardized, and moving through predictable channels, from production to customer. The primary concerns are manufacturing lead times, distribution efficiency, and meeting production demands with speed and scale. Products are usually uniform in configuration, supported by a clean bill of materials, and optimized for high-volume flow.

In contrast, SPSCM deals with the product after it has been sold and deployed, often under unique, unpredictable conditions. The product now exists in various configurations depending on customer-specific customizations, age, and wear. Support may involve parts that are no longer manufactured, legacy versions, or refurbished components. The focus is no longer on speed to market, but speed to resolution—ensuring uptime, availability, and risk mitigation. Here, the product is a system-in-use, potentially regulated, mission-critical, or operating under warranty or service contracts.

Another important difference is in the visibility and traceability requirements. In FSCM, tracking ends once the product is delivered to the customer or partner. SPSCM, on the other hand, requires ongoing visibility into the product's condition, usage patterns, failure rates, and repair history. This data is vital for ensuring the right part is delivered for the specific product configuration, avoiding SLA violations and costly delays. Additionally, the physical condition of the product in SPSCM can vary widely, requiring triage and diagnosis to identify which part has failed.

Moreover, the volume and velocity of product movement are entirely different. Forward supply chains benefit from batching, economies of scale, and planning production schedules. SPSCM must operate under conditions of fragmented, low-volume, and high-urgency demand—often requiring expedited shipments, just-in-case inventory, and strategic stocking across global service locations.

Product Differences

	Forward Supply Chain	Service Parts Supply Chain
Product Status	New, unused	In-use, aged, possibly modified
Configuration	Standardized, consistent	Customized, varied by customer, usage, and upgrades
Volume	High-volume production & distribution	Low-volume, high-mix demand for individual parts
Support Window	Unit product delivery or end of warranty	Extends through product life and post-sales years
Data Requirements	Demand forecasts, lead times, inventory turnover	Failure data, installed base tracking, service history
Fulfillment Priority	Cost effective, scale	Uptime, speed, SLA compliance

Characteristics of Products Within the SPSCM Model

The types of products SPSCM supports within a particular supply chain are tied closely and influenced by the product lifecycle itself. These include:

Product Lifecycle	Duration	Product types	Characteristics
Short	1-3 years	Consumer electronics (e.g., cell phones, laptops)	▪ Steep ramp-up stage ▪ Short maturity and sustaining stage ▪ Rapid decline stage
Medium	5-10 years	HVAC systems, data center infrastructure, appliances	▪ Gradual ramp stages ▪ Extended maturity stages ▪ Slow decline stages
Long	10 + years	Heavy machinery, capital equipment, aerospace, medical	▪ Lower volume and long duration of ramp ▪ In active production for years ▪ Decades long service support requirements

Short Lifecycle Products

Products that have short lifecycles are typically in industries with frequent new product launches. SPSCM support for these products typically last only through the warranty and extended service agreements, which usually end a few years after product shipment, as most customers transition to newer versions.

For most Original Equipment Manufacturers (OEMs), multiple products or product revisions are released each year as newer technologies emerge. Within each model type, there are often configuration options to choose from (e.g., cell phone case, hard drive size). Adding to the complexity, new product launches frequently overlap with ongoing support for previous products, requiring simultaneous lifecycle management with varying service level agreement (SLA) requirements.

Complexities of short lifecycle management:

- **High volume repair and refurbishment**
  - *Example:* I supported a customer managing centralized cell phone repairs, handling 10,000 repairs per week.
- **Early and bulk service parts procurement**
  - Many parts must be purchased early in the lifecycle, often before product shipments or clear demand trends emerge.
  - Most parts are low-cost, but small forecasting errors can lead to excessive and expensive inventory exposure.
- **Highly volatile sales forecasts**
- **Unpredictable user induced damage, making demand difficult to forecast**
  - Can vary by product configuration (e.g., Standard versus Pro versions).
- **Variations in failure rates among product models**
  - *Example:* A laptop manufacturer releasing multiple models annually may initially estimate uniform failure rates for parts. However, after sales ramp up, one model may experience unexpectedly high failure rates, leading to inventory depletion, supply chain disruptions, and extended supplier lead times.

While centralizing service repair operations helps streamline inventory management, balancing inventory needs, and repair volume remains a significant challenge in short-lifecycle environments.

Product Failure Rate

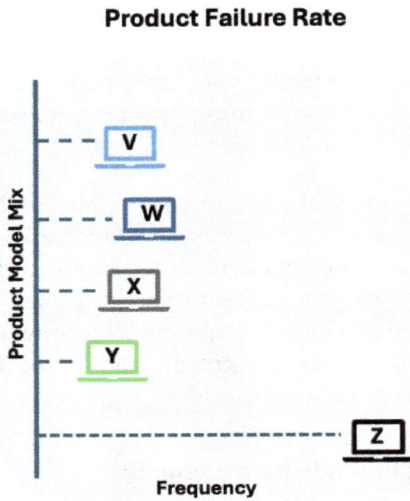

Medium Lifecycle Products

These industries require robust warranty and service contract support as the post-sales support requirements have a longer duration than the short-lifecycle products.

Due to the semi-permanent or permanent nature, ongoing field support is often required, introducing additional layers of complexity. Maintenance activities are frequently carried out by:

- Independent service providers
- Dealers
- Distributor networks
- Affiliated entities working on behalf of the OEM

Each of these stakeholders typically maintains its own service parts inventory, making alignment across all parties crucial for efficient service delivery.

To address these complexities, OEMs must plan inventory across an extensive network, incorporating both their own inventory and service provider support orders. Accurately identifying true demand is challenging, as many service providers don't always report product failures. Instead, parts orders from the providers are often intended to replenish their own inventory networks, which may be spread across fixed warehouses and service vehicles.

Challenges in Medium Lifecycle Product Management:

- **Managing multiple product lines with thousands of parts**
  - High part commonality between product models and revisions
  - True demand is difficult to determine when service providers are involved.
- **Coordinating a large network of inventory locations**
  - While often regional, these networks can be global, adding complexity.
- **Ensuring long-term service availability after production ceases**
  - Suppliers of service parts may discontinue production, requiring OEMs to find alternative sources.

Long Lifecycle Products

Industries such as semiconductor manufacturing systems, capital equipment, heavy machinery, and aerospace are characterized by exceptionally long product lifecycles and fewer annual new product launches. While these extended lifecycles allow for strategic planning, they also pose risks such as excess inventory accumulation due to inefficient SPSCM operations.

Common Challenges in Long-Lifecycle Industries:

- **Low inventory turnover and frequent write-offs**
  - Many critical parts are large, expensive, and infrequently used but must be available as speculative inventory.
- **Support requirements spanning decades across multiple product generations**
- **Maintaining a reliable, long-term supplier base**
- **Slow-moving, high-cost parts create financial burdens**
- **Institutional knowledge loss due to workforce attrition**
  - Product support often outlasts employee tenure, leading to knowledge gaps.

Company Background

A global company manufactures agricultural machinery—tractors, combines, and harvesters—used by farmers around the world. The company manages both the forward production and delivery of new equipment and the ongoing distribution of service parts for decades-long support.

Scenario Overview

FSCM – Centralized, Planned Point of Supply

When launching a new tractor model, the company's forward supply chain operates through centralized production facilities located in key countries with high manufacturing capacity and low production costs.

For these plants, units are shipped to regional distribution centers (RDCs), then to dealers or directly to large farm operations. The point of supply is strategically consolidated to:

- Leverage economies of scale
- Optimize production schedules
- Minimize unit costs and lead times

The movement of goods follows a linear, planned route with high predictability. Locations and volumes are known in advance, allowing for predicable sourcing and replacement.

SPSCM – Decentralized, Responsive Point of Supply

After the tractors are sold and deployed globally, they require ongoing support through the SPSCM. Over the equipment's twenty-to-thirty-year lifecycle, replacement parts are required in remote rural areas across different continents, often in urgent, seasonal windows (e.g., during harvest).

To meet this need:

- The company must maintain service parts inventories in a wide network of local depots, dealers, or third-party logistics providers.

- Some parts must be pre-positioned at smaller, rural service points even amid uncertain demand, simply to maintain service-level agreements.
- Reverse logistics (e.g., refurbished components) are also used as part of the supply strategy.

Unlike the predictable structure of FSCM, SPSCM's point of supply is decentralized and dynamically adapted to:

- Local failure rates
- Geographic dispersion
- Service urgency
- Product age

This shift from centralized bulk delivery (FSCM) to localized, sometimes on-demand, stocking (SPSCM) introduces greater complexity in planning, cost, and execution.

Operational Outcomes

To succeed:

- FSCM optimizes around a few high-capacity supply points.
- SPSCM must support hundreds or thousands of micro-fulfillment points, even if volume is low but the criticality is high.

For instance, a $10 sensor may need to be stocked in a rural depot in Brazil for a single tractor because a failure could halt an entire harvest.

Chapter 5

Difference #4:
Type of Demand and How It's Forecasted

Introduction

In supply chain management, accurately forecasting demand is fundamental to aligning supply with customer expectations, minimizing inventory costs, and ensuring operational efficiency. However, the nature of that demand—and the way it is forecasted—varies significantly between FSCM and SPSCM. While both rely on prediction models, the sourcing, timing, and behavior of demand are fundamentally different, requiring distinct planning strategies and execution frameworks.

FSCM is primarily focused on fulfilling product demand driven by market-facing factors such as sales forecasts, product launches, and seasonal promotions. Its forecasts are typically structured, proactive, and based on well-established commercial patterns. In contrast, SPSCM deals with reactive demand—stemming from equipment failures, maintenance schedules, and service obligations—often long after the initial sale. This type of demand is harder to predict, dispersed across a wide geography, and tightly linked to an expanding installed base. As a result, SPSCM must rely on sophisticated, data-intensive models that account for uncertainty, part failure behaviors, and service level requirements. Understanding these differences is key to designing resilient and responsive supply chains tailored to their specific roles.

Topics Covered in This Chapter:

- **Type of Demand: Forward Supply Chain versus SPSCM**
- **Demand Forecasting in Forward Supply Chain Management**
- **Demand Forecasting in SPSCM**
- **Summary: Use Case Example – Global Manufacturer of Commercial HVAC Systems**

Type of Demand: Forward Supply Chain versus SPSCM

In practice, there are two fundamental types of demand that drive FSCM operations: **product demand** and **component/raw material demand**.

Product demand refers to the market-facing need for finished goods—the items that the customer purchases. It is the primary driver that determines the overall direction and tempo of the supply chain. This demand is typically independent and largely predictable, influenced by customer purchases, sales forecasts, product launches, and marketing promotions. It reflects new product acquisition and flows linearly from producers to end-users or retailers. Because it is closely tied to commercial planning and consumer behavior, FSCM demand patterns often exhibit seasonal trends, promotion spikes, or growth curves aligned with the early product lifecycle stages—particularly launch and growth. Accurate forecasting of product demand is critical, as it lays the foundation for all upstream planning activities.

Components and raw materials demand, by contrast, represents the internal operational need for the inputs required to manufacture finished goods. This type of demand is derived directly from product demand using the **Manufacturing Bill of Materials (MBOM)**. For every forecasted unit of product, FSCM planning calculates how much of each raw material or component is needed to meet production targets. As such, component demand is **dependent demand**, fully reliant on the accuracy and timing of product demand forecasts.

The interaction between these two types of demand is tightly coupled and sequential. If product demand increases due to a market surge, component demand must also ramp up—often on short notice. Conversely, overestimating product demand can result in surplus inventory of both finished goods and raw materials, leading to high carry costs. Therefore, any forecasting inaccuracies ripple through the supply chain. Effective FSCM relies on synchronizing both demand streams through integrated planning systems, agile procurement, and continuous monitoring of market signals.

Attribute	Product Demand	Component / Raw Material Demand
Definition	Demand for finished goods from end customers	Demand for parts/materials needed for production
Type of Demand	Independent	Dependent (derived from product demand)
Driven By	Market needs, forecasts, and customer orders	Product demand and the MBOM
Flexibility	Variable, influenced by external factors	Calculated from product demand forecasts

In contrast, SPSCM operates primarily on dependent and often intermittent demand. The need for spare parts arises not from new purchases, but from failures, wear, or routine maintenance of products already in use. This makes SPSCM demand reactive and service-based, influenced by environmental conditions, usage variability, the age of the installed base, and geographic distribution. Unlike forward demand, which can be stimulated through marketing, **SPSCM demand is passive—it cannot be artificially created and must be anticipated through detailed planning**.

While FSCM demand typically enjoys relative volume consistency, SPSCM must handle "lumpy" or sporadic requirements that resist traditional forecasting models. This distinction significantly impacts inventory strategy, replenishment methods, and performance metrics within SPSCM.

Another important difference lies in the timing and urgency of demand. FSCM demand often works with longer lead times—factories and distributors can operate on structured production and delivery schedules. SPSCM, on the other hand, operates under compressed timelines. Customers need parts quickly to reduce downtime or meet service-level agreements (SLAs). Consequently, SPSCM requires pre-positioned inventory, rapid fulfillment capabilities, and real-time demand sensing.

The stakeholders that initiate demand also differ. FSCM demand is typically driven by sales, marketing, or procurement teams. SPSCM demand often originates from field service technicians, customer support centers, or end-users responding to immediate service needs. This necessitates strong integration with service organizations and the ability to respond to granular event-based signals.

As discussed in the previous chapter on product lifecycles, FSCM demand trends remain relatively stable within the product's sales and manufacturing window. Once a product is discontinued, material requirements end and the focus shifts to newer product releases. Over time, this creates a "sawtooth" pattern—each product has a distinct start and end point in the manufacturing lifecycle.

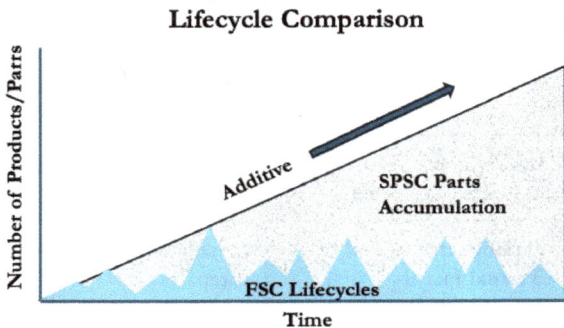

Lifecycle Comparison

Number of Products/Parts

Additive

SPSC Parts Accumulation

FSC Lifecycles

Time

In contrast, SPSCM demand extends well beyond the end of manufacturing. As more products are introduced, SPSCM experiences a cumulative effect, where service demand increases due to a growing installed base and extended product support requirements—especially for long-lifecycle products. This accumulation means that, while FSCM demand requirements fluctuate with manufacturing cycles, SPSCM demand fluctuates with product launches and continually grows, requiring management of a broader and aging portfolio of parts and products.

Type of Demand – FSCM versus SPSCM

	Forward Supply Chain	Service Parts Supply Chain
Type of Demand	Independent, driven by new product purchases	Dependent, driven by equipment failures and maintenance
Trigger for Demand	Sales activity, product launches, customer orders	Usage conditions, failure rates, service schedules
Pattern	Predictable, smooth, seasonal or trend-based	Sporadic and irregular
Customer Behavior	Influenced by marketing, pricing, and promotions	Influenced by repair needs and service level expectations
Timing of Demand	Pre-sale or point-of-sale	Post-sale, often years after initial launch
Forecasting Challenge	Moderate – based on historical trends	High – requires complex modeling and probabilistic tools

Demand Forecasting in FSCM

Since the goal of FSCM is to supply new products into retail, distribution, or B2B channels, demand tends to follow product launch cycles, promotional efforts, and competitive positioning. As a result, FSCM demand forecasts can often be developed months or even quarters in advance with relatively stable accuracy—especially for high-volume, fast-moving goods. This relationship allows FSCM to operate proactively, optimizing inventory levels, production schedules, and transportation planning around sales targets.

FSCM demand is heavily influenced by channel dynamics. Retailers, distributors, and regional sales teams provide demand inputs based on their local knowledge, shelf space requirements, and promotional calendars. These inputs are aggregated and analyzed to create a centralized demand plan (e.g., Sales & Operations Plan (S&OP)), which serves as the foundation for production and distribution decisions. Effective demand management in FSCM also involves demand shaping—the use of pricing strategies, promotions, or bundling to influence customer purchasing behavior in alignment with supply constraints.

Finally, modern FSCM increasingly leverages real-time sales and consumption data to fine-tune supply planning. Approaches like time-series forecasting—using historical records, demand sensing, and POS data feeds—allow companies to reduce forecast error and adjust quickly to shifts in consumer behavior. In this context, the forward supply chain serves not only as a logistics function but also as a strategic enabler of sales growth and market responsiveness.

Attribute	Forward Supply Chain Management
Demand Timing	Proactive, planned in advance
Lifecycle Sensitivity	Closely aligned with product sales lifecycle
Forecast Drivers	Historical sales, seasonal trends, marketing campaigns
Demand Planning Tools	Time series algorithms, S&OP, POS data, sales input integration
Channel Influence	Strong—retailers, distributors, and regional sales inform demand plans

FSCM Forecasting Product to Inbound Raw Materials and Components

In FSCM, inbound components and raw materials represent a critical form of derived demand—that is, demand that stems from the need to manufacture finished goods in response to market sales and forecasts. These inputs, which include raw materials, subassemblies, and specialized components, are not consumed by end customers directly but are essential for creating the products that will be. This type of demand is intrinsically linked to the production schedule and is heavily influenced by product design, the MBOM, and manufacturing strategy (e.g., make-to-stock versus make-to-order).

Managing inbound demand in FSCM requires a high degree of synchronization across suppliers, manufacturers, and logistics providers. Material requirements planning (MRP) and enterprise resource planning (ERP) systems are typically employed to convert finished product forecasts into precise orders for upstream materials. The accuracy and timing of these inbound orders are vital for maintaining product efficiency, minimizing inventory hold costs, and avoiding stockouts that could disrupt the entire supply chain.

Furthermore, the predictability of inbound demand in FSCM is generally higher than in service parts supply chains. This is because the demand for finished goods is typically forecastable using historical sales data, market trends, and promotional calendars—allowing planners to estimate with relative confidence the volume and timing of required materials. Nonetheless, complexities arise in environments with high product variability, long lead times, or supply base fragmentation, where a single delayed component can stall entire production lines.

Another key distinction regarding FSCM forecast complexity being more predictable is that in most cases—but not all—forecasts for raw materials and components are directly linked to a particular manufacturing location. Product sales forecasts and site-specific manufacturing capacity constraints, along with MBOM requirements for each product—which is known—simplifies the forecasting process in FSCM.

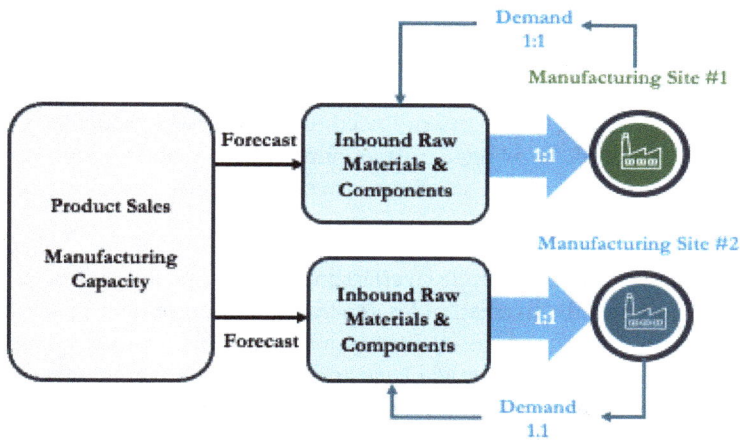

Demand Forecasting in SPSCM

Forecasting demand in the SPSCM environment presents a unique set of challenges that distinguish it from traditional forward supply chain forecasting. Unlike the relatively predictable and structured product demand in FSCM, SPSCM demand is driven by part failure rates, usage rates, environmental conditions, and the aging of the installed product base. These variables make

SPSCM demand highly irregular, intermittent, and often non-linear, rendering many conventional forecasting models ineffective.

When products are in the field—like with vehicles, medical devices, industrial equipment, or electronics—they experience wear and degradation over time. This leads to the need for replacements, repairs, or maintenance, which generates demand for service parts. Demand is reactive and highly variable, rooted in product performance and reliability data.

One core challenge in forecasting SPSCM demand lies in the inherent uncertainty in part failure rates. While manufacturers may have some historical data or reliability metrics, real-world conditions vary widely by customer, geography, and usage intensity. Two identical machines may experience different failure timelines due to factors such as operating environment, user behavior, or maintenance practices. This makes it difficult to apply a standard predictive model, leading to forecast variability and often requiring probabilistic approaches such as failure rate modeling or condition-based maintenance planning.

Another major difficulty arises from the long tail of parts. SPSCM often supports a vast number of low-volume, low-frequency parts—some of which may not be needed for years. Forecasting such "lumpy" or "slow-moving" demand is statistically complex, especially for parts where historical usage data is limited or nonexistent. These parts still need to be available, particularly in industries with strict SLAs or regulatory requirements, creating a high stakes forecasting environment where stockouts are costly and overstocking ties up capital and storage.

SPSCM is also affected by lifecycle overlap and product proliferation. As new product models enter the market, older generations often remain in service. Forecasting must therefore account for not just the single product's support requirements, but the entire installed base and its evolving maintenance needs. Additionally, parts may be shared across multiple products or uniquely tied to one version, further complicating the forecasting process.

Finally, external events and service behaviors—such as recalls, field upgrades, policy changes, or shifts in service strategies—can create sudden and unplanned demand spikes. Service organizations, often the initiators of part requests, may not always communicate future needs in a structured or timely way, reducing forecast visibility and increasing the need for responsive planning systems.

Attribute	Effect on SPSCM Forecasting
Part Failure Rate Variability	Leads to unpredictable, non-linear demand; requires probabilistic or reliability-based models

Attribute	Effect on SPSCM Forecasting
Low-Frequency, Long-Tail Demand	Makes statistical forecasting difficult; many parts have sparse or no historical usage data
Lifecycle Overlap	Increases complexity, by requiring simultaneous support for multiple product generations
Installed Base Growth	Expands demand volume and variability over time as more products enter the service pool
Forecasting Horizon	Often longer and less defined; demand may persist years after manufacturing ends

Unlike FSCM, SPSCM teams operate under a much higher degree of demand uncertainty due to the inherently unpredictable nature of part failures. Instead of relying on direct sales signals, SPSCM must anticipate when and how often service parts will fail. Forecasting in this context is driven by analyzing historical part usage data, which is then projected forward using advanced statistics and algorithms to estimate future demand as accurately as possible.

Similar to how FSCM uses sales forecast and production constraints to predict future needs for components, raw materials, and finished goods, SPSCM also relies on a combination of key inputs to shape its forecasts. These inputs typically include:

- Product sales forecasts (as a proxy for future installed base size)
- Product lifecycle stage (to estimate failure patterns over time)
- Installed base locations and expected growth rates
- Type and scope of service entitlements (e.g., warranty coverage, service-level agreements, extended support contracts)

However, a key difference lies in the geographical dispersion of demand sources. While FSCM typically concentrates manufacturing-related demand forecasts around a few centralized production facilities, SPSCM must account for demand originating from hundreds or even thousands of locations where the products are deployed. Each of these locations represents a potential failure point, making demand forecasting highly decentralized and variable.

For organizations that support aggressive SLAs—such as guaranteed part delivery within two hours—SPSCM cannot depend solely on shipping service parts from a central warehouse. To meet these stringent service levels, a complex, multi-echelon inventory network is required. This network involves strategically placed inventory at various levels—from national distribution centers to regional hubs and even forward-stocking locations—so that service parts are always within close proximity to the installed base.

In essence, the multi-echelon inventory network serves as a dynamic buffer between parts procurement and field demand. While it enables rapid response, it significantly increases the complexity of forecasting compared to FSCM. Each node in the network must be forecast independently, factoring in location failure rates, service agreements, and replenishment lead times—making SPSCM forecasting not only more uncertain but also exponentially more complex.

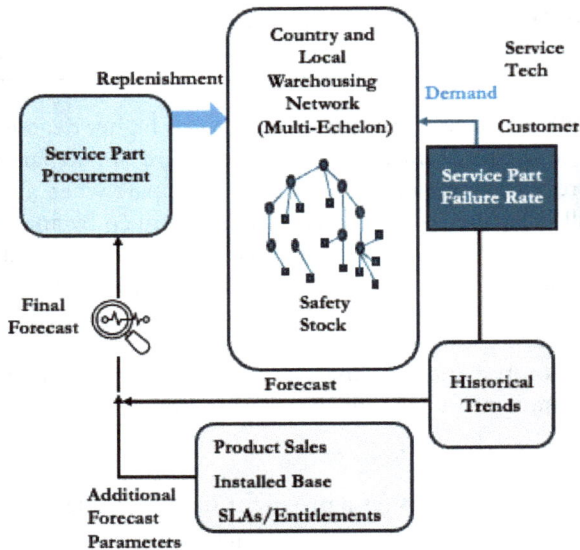

Summary

FSCM operates on two tightly linked demand types: independent product demand driven by customer purchases, and dependent component demand derived from production planning. Accurate forecasting is essential to ensure synchronization between them. In contrast, the SPSCM is driven by dependent, intermittent demand arising from maintenance and repair needs long after the product sale. While FSCM demand is predictable and can be shaped through marketing and promotion, SPSCM demand is reactive, urgent, and harder to forecast. While FSCM demand fades once a product is discontinued, SPSCM demand accumulates over time, requiring long-term support across multiple product generations.

SPSCM forecasting is challenged by variable part failure rates, low-frequency demand patterns, product lifecycle overlap, and unpredictable service events. It must rely on probabilistic and responsive approaches to manage high uncertainty and ensure part availability. This creates a delicate balance between service continuity and cost control, making forecasting both critical and complex.

SPSCM must anticipate part failures that are distributed across a vast, decentralized installed base. Forecasting in SPSCM requires advanced analytics that integrate product lifecycle data, installed base growth, service entitlements, and historical failure rates. The added need to support high-service-level agreements through multi-echelon inventory networks further increases complexity, requiring granular, location-specific forecasting. This dynamic and reactive nature of SPSCM forecasting contrasts sharply with the structured, proactive forecasting model used in FSCM.

Chapter Summary Use Case:
Global Manufacturer of Commercial HVAC Systems

Company Background

A multinational company manufactures commercial HVAC (Heating, Ventilation, and Air Conditioning) units for large buildings, hospitals, and factories. Its operations span both forward supply chain manufacturing and after-market service support across North America, Europe, and Asia.

Scenario Overview

FSCM – Demand Source and Predictability

When the company introduces a new HVAC unit, demand forecasting in the forward supply chain is primarily tied to new product sales. Forecasts are developed based on:

- Historical sales data for similar models
- Market research and competitor activity
- Sales promotions and channel commitments
- Seasonal construction cycles (e.g., summer spikes)

The forward supply chain benefits from a reasonably high level of predictability. Orders come in batches, lead times are planned months in

---

advance, and production can be scheduled accordingly. Demand variability exists, but it is largely managed through sales planning and channel inventory buffers.

Service Parts Supply Chain (SPSCM) – Demand Source and Predictability:

Once HVAC systems are installed in the field, the SPSCM takes over. Over the next fifteen-to-twenty years, the company must supply thousands of replacement parts—compressors, capacitors, sensors, filters, control boards—across its service network.

Demand here is driven by part failures, not new purchases. Predictability is a challenge due to:

- Operating environments differences (e.g., dusty factory versus clean hospital)
- Variability in maintenance quality
- Component reliability variations
- Unexpected repair needs from emergency failures

Even though some failure trends can be modeled using **Mean Time Between Failure (MTBF)** or predictive analytics, the timing and volume of demand are far more sporadic. For example, a single power surge could cause a regional spike in compressor replacements—something that wouldn't be visible in traditional sales-driven forecasting models.

Outcome and Operational Differences

To cope with these two different supply chain profiles:

- FSCM uses centralized forecasting, manufacturing-to-stock strategies, and batch logistics based on anticipated sales volumes.
- SPSCM, in contrast, uses decentralized planning, tiered inventory stocking models, and just-in-case stocking strategies at service hubs to deal with sporadic urgent demand patterns.

Furthermore, failure-based demand often persists for ten-to-fifteen years after the original product has been discontinued, requiring careful obsolescence management and last-time-buy decisions, which has no equivalent in the forward supply chain.

Key Lessons from the Use Case

Attribute	FSCM	SPSCM
Demand	Predictable & proactive	Reactive and variable
Demand Stems From	Planned deployments	Unplanned failures

Chapter 6

Difference #5:
Inventory Variety, Volume, and Network Structure

Introduction

Inventory is a central pillar of supply chain strategy. Its location, classification, and purpose significantly influence a supply chain's ability to fulfill demand efficiently and cost-effectively. In this chapter, we will explore the characteristics of inventory and examine foundational inventory states, followed by a comparison of the inventory structures of FSCM and SPSCM. While both models rely on inventory to meet customer expectations, the nature of the inventory, timing of the demand, and service requirements create fundamental differences in how inventory is managed.

Variety and Volume of Unique Inventory Support

A key difference between FSCM and the SPSCM lies in the breadth of individual parts numbers that need to be managed.

Within FSCM, physical inventory exists in two main states: raw materials and components necessary for product manufacturing, and finished goods.

The raw materials and components required for production are outlined in the **Manufacturing BOM (MBOM)**—a document that details all necessary material inputs for a given product. All materials must be present in precise quantities during manufacturing. If the product is discontinued, the need for its materials ceases. This creates a one-to-one dependency: all or nothing. As a result, the number of unique material part numbers is limited to those products currently in production.

Similarly, finished goods in the FSC consist of a defined number of **Stock Keeping Units (SKUs)**, aligned to the active product lineup in the marketplace.

In contrast, the SPSC supports a much broader and more complex variety of parts due to the multi-generational support of products over an extended lifecycle.

Inventory variety in the SPSC is driven by the **Service Parts Bill of Materials (SPBOM)**—a targeted subset of the MBOM. The SPBOM identifies all **Field Replaceable Units (FRUs)**—components likely to fail and subject to replacement. These must be forecasted, sourced, and stocked to meet replacement demands after the product has been delivered. However, the MBOM-SPBOM relationship is not always one-to-one:

- In FSCM: A mechanical engine may be sourced as a complete unit from a single supplier and tracked under one part number.
- In SPSCM: The same engine is decomposed into multiple FRUs, each with its own failure profile and part number, requiring individualized service planning.

Terminology Note:

- The term *"Field Replaceable Unit (FRU)* is used interchangeably with *"part"* or *"service part."*
- This distinction is reintroduced only when clarity is required.

This SPBOM process can result in hundreds of FRUs for a single assembly and thousands across a product line—requiring evaluation for sourcing, stocking, and planning within SPSCM operations.

Moreover, because SPBOMs target serviceable and repairable parts (not raw materials or whole assemblies), their supplier base often differs from those used in manufacturing. As such, procurement channels for service parts may not overlap with production procurement.

Inventory Location Point Differences in FSCM and SPSCM

Another key inventory difference is in the number and configuration of inventory locations.

In FSCM, inventory flows in a linear progression from the supplier to the customer. Key inventory stages include:

1. **Raw Material & Component Inventory**: Basic inputs held at supplier sites or the manufacturing plant
2. **Work-in-Progress (WIP) Inventory**: Semi-finished goods on the production floor.
3. **Finished Goods Inventory**: Completed products stored in central warehouses awaiting shipment
4. **Customer Inventory (Retail/Distributor)**: Goods at downstream partners' locations before final sale

Forward Supply Chain Inventory State & Locations

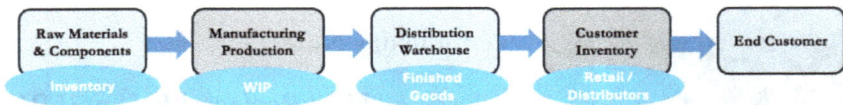

The goal within FSCM is to hold just enough inventory to support manufacturing and sales—lean, efficient, and optimized based on production capacity, forecasted demand, and warehouse targets. Just-in-Time (JIT) models exemplify this ideal.

In contrast, SPSCM inventory exists to ensure rapid part availability for field service. Its demand is erratic, urgent, and geographically dispersed. Inventory states include:

1. **Centralized Service Parts Inventory**: Global distribution centers storing high-value or slow-moving parts
2. **Regional Depots**: Intermediate warehouses supporting local markets
3. **Field Stocking Locations (FSLs):** Near-service zones, holding fast-moving or SLA-critical parts
4. **Technician-Truck Inventory**: Parts carried by field engineers for immediate use
5. **Reverse Inventory (Returns, Repair, Core Parts)**: Returned or reconditioned parts entered back into circulation

SPSC inventory is designed for availability, not efficiency. **Stock must be positioned where it might be needed—not just where it's economical to store.** We'll explore these complexities further in the next section on multi-echelon SPSC networks.

Service Parts Supply Chain Inventory State & Locations

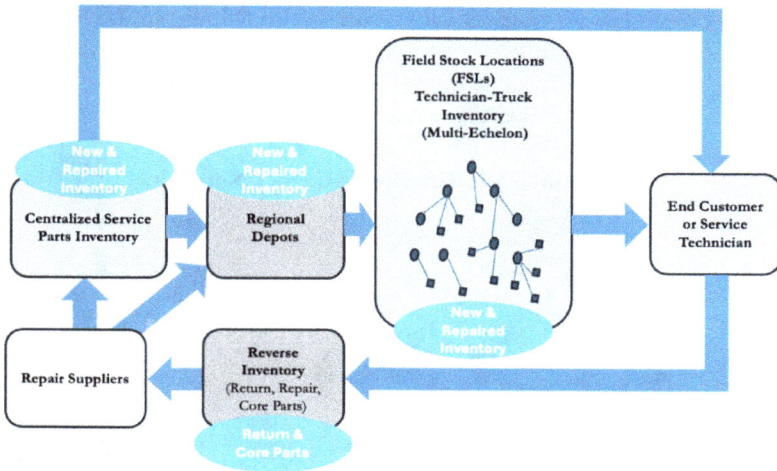

Comparing FSCM and SPSCM Network Structures

FSCM networks are typically centralized and linear. Demand originates at the manufacturing stage, so raw materials and components are shipped directly to plants. Finished goods are then moved to central distribution hubs, and eventually to retail or customer sites. This unidirectional flow is optimized for cost efficiency and scale.

FSCM Raw Material and Components Inventory Locations
(Suppliers Ship to Limited Manufacturing Locations)

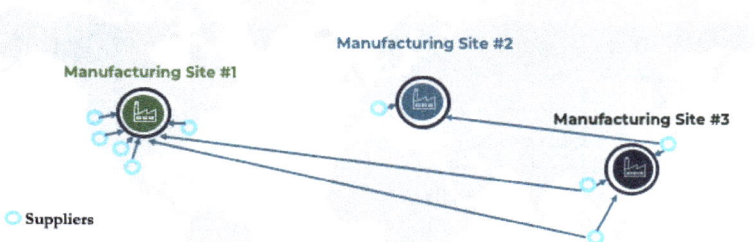

SPSCM networks, in contrast, are decentralized and multi-echelon. Demand originates at the point of failure—wherever the product is in use globally. The network is designed to move inventory closer to the failure point, reducing downtime. It features multiple inventory layers (central, regional, local, mobile) to buffer against uncertainty. The inclusion of reverse logistics adds complexity and creates a continuous forward-reverse inventory loop.

SPSCM Multi-Echelon Inventory Network

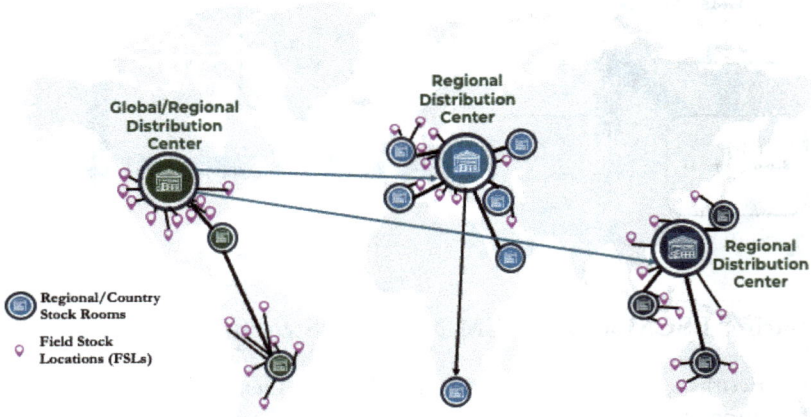

SPSCM operations must implement multi-echelon inventory optimization (MEIO) to balance high availability with cost constraints—an inherently more complex challenge than typical FSCM logistics.

Inventory Comparisons Between the FSCM and SPSCM

Attribute	FSCM	SPSCM
Inventory Objective	Minimize cost and maximize turnover	Maximize availability and responsiveness
Inventory State Types	Raw materials, WIP, finished goods, and retail	Central stock, regional depot, FSLs, technician inventory, and returns
Network Structure	Centralized and linear	Decentralized and multi-echelon
Inventory Movement	Uni-directional (supplier to customer)	Bi-directional (forward and reverse logistics)

Attribute	FSCM	SPSCM
Optimization Focus	Cost efficiency, bulk fulfillment	SLA compliance, downtime minimization

Closing Summary

The differences in inventory variety, volume, and network structure between the FSCM and SPSCM are not merely operational—they are strategic as well. FSCMs leans toward efficiency and is optimized for planning production and predictable demand. The SPSCM network, by contrast, requires flexibility, redundancy, and a broader inventory profile to ensure service continuity in the face of failure. Designing and managing these two inventory systems requires fundamentally different approaches, technologies, and metrics for success.

Chapter Summary Use Case:
MEScan Inc. – FSC and SPSC Inventory Strategy in Practice

Company Overview

MEScan Inc. is a global leader in the design and manufacturing of advanced medical imaging systems, such as MRI, CT, and PET scanners. These systems are capital-intensive, mission-critical assets for hospitals and diagnostic clinics, with stringent service uptime requirements. MEScan's operations span both **FSCM** and **SPSCM** networks—each optimized for different objectives.

Phase 1: MBOM Development and FSCM Procurement Strategy

MBOM Creation

For its newest MRI model, MEScan engineers created a **Manufacturing Bill of Materials (MBOM)**. The MBOM includes:

- Mechanical components (chassis, housing, gantry arm)
- High-precision electromechanical subassemblies (RF coils, patient tables, gradient amplifiers)
- Embedded systems (real-time control processors, firmware)
- Cooling systems and cryogenics
- Cabling and connectors
- Final packaging materials

Each component is tied to a specific part number, supplier, and required manufacturing process.

FSC Procurement Process

- **Tier-1** Suppliers provide electromechanical and digital subassemblies, often pre-tested and packaged.
- **Tier-2/3** Suppliers provide raw materials (copper wiring, steel, aluminum casings).
- All parts are delivered to one or two global manufacturing plants in North America and Europe.

MEScan uses a JIT model where suppliers deliver components based on the production schedule. Inventory is held for minimal durations, tracking through centralized ERP systems.

- Raw materials and WIP are staged in tightly controlled zones on the factory floor.
- Finished scanners are sent to regional distribution centers.
- Installation and commissioning teams work with hospitals to deploy the equipment.

Phase 2: SPBOM Development and SPSCM Procurement Strategy

SPBOM Creation

Post-manufacture, MEScan's SPSCM experts and product engineering create a **Service Parts Bill of Materials (SPBOM)** from the MBOM. This process involves:

- Reviewing each MBOM component to determine serviceability
- Identifying Field Replaceable Units (FRUs) that:
  - o Have a high probability of failure or wear over time
  - o Are technically feasible for field replacement
  - o Are economically viable to stock and repair

The original MBOM with approximately 900 components, including hundreds of assemblies mostly sourced as complete units. The SPBOM identifies ~2,000 unique FRUs, including:

- Power supply boards
- Cooling modules
- Firmware control units
- User interface touchscreens
- Shielding cabling and sensors
- Pneumatic actuators and valves

- O-rings, screw, washers, and fittings

Each FRU is assigned a service-specific part number.

SPSCM Procurement Process

- Some FRUs are sourced from the same Tier-1 suppliers as the MBOM.
- Others come from third-party or aftermarket suppliers who specialize in service-grade or remanufactured components.
- Strategic sourcing contracts are signed for multi-year support and replenishment.
- In many cases, remanufactured parts from reverse logistics channels (returned and repaired FRUs) are added to the pool.

SPSCM operates under different procurement logic.

- Procurement is based on failure rate modeling, installed base geography, and SLA targets—not production schedules.
- Safety stock and reorder points are calculated using **Multi-Echelon Inventory Optimization (MEIO)** algorithms.

Phase 3: SPSCM Inventory Staging Across the Multi-Echelon Network

MEScan builds a multi-layered inventory architecture to support post-sales across seventy countries:

- **Central Distribution Centers (CDC)**
  - Located in North America and Europe
  - Store slow-moving, high-value parts (e.g., control computers, RF amplifiers)
  - Replenish downstream locations
  - Include testing, configuration, and repair labs for returned units

- **Regional Depots**
  - Located in major cities (e.g., Frankfurt, Dubai, Singapore, São Paulo)
  - Stock medium-moving parts tailored to regional installed base.

- o Serves as a buffer against supply chain disruptions or customs delays

- **Field Stocking Locations (FSLs)**
  - o Strategically placed within one to three hours of dense hospital clusters
  - o Stock fast-moving parts such as touch panels, sensors, and connectors
  - o Linked to predictive analytics systems that forecast regional parts usage

- **Technician-Truck Inventory**
  - o Service technicians carry service parts based on their assigned geography and equipment mix.
  - o Parts are optimized monthly based on past service calls, weather, seasonality, and new product introductions.

- **Reverse Logistics & Repair Loop**
  - o Defective FRUs are returned from the field to repair hubs.
  - o Usable parts are cleaned, re-tested, and re-entered into CDC inventory.
  - o Core part tracking (e.g., for MRI gradient amplifiers) ensures environmental and cost compliance.

From this use case, it becomes apparent that MEScan's FSCM and SPSCM organizations operate as interdependent but functionally distinct systems. MEScan successfully leverages two inventory architectures:

- A **centralized, lean, JIT-focused supply chain** built around predictable manufacturing demand
- A **decentralized, highly responsive, multi-echelon SPSCM** structure designed to ensure availability, uptime, and long-term customer satisfaction

Part 2: Overview

Key Challenges in Service Parts Supply Chain Management

Introduction: The Five Core Challenges of SPSCM

SPSCM sits at the intersection of customer urgency, product complexity, and operational unpredictability. Unlike traditional supply chains, which are largely structured around linear production flows and predictable consumption patterns, SPSCM must support installed products long after initial sale—often across decades, geographies, and support models. This creates a distinct set of challenges that traditional planning systems and supply strategies are not designed to handle.

To effectively manage this environment, supply chain professionals must navigate five foundational challenges that shape the performance, cost, and responsiveness of the service network:

1. **Diversity of Service Models** – No two service programs are alike. Some customers purchase premium support packages with strict uptime SLAs, while others rely on pay-per-use or no-contract support. This wide variation in service commitments, geographic coverage, and parts entitlements complicates standardization efforts and requires tailored inventory and support strategies.

2. **Dynamics of SPSCM Demand Forecasting** – Predicting demand for service parts is not only more uncertain than in forward manufacturing, but also fundamentally different. Forecasts must account for sporadic failures, varying usage rates, and unpredictable return patterns. Historical demand is often an unreliable indicator, forcing planners to rely on alternative signals like installed base analytics and failure-rate modeling.

3. **OEM Field Repair and Maintenance Multi-Echelon Network** – Supporting global customers requires a layered inventory network—from central distribution centers to regional depots to forward-stocking locations and even technician trunks. Managing this complex, multi-

tiered architecture becomes especially difficult in capital-intensive industries like semiconductor manufacturing, where parts are expensive, bulky, and required in remote geographies with limited logistics support.

4. **Inventory Control** – The high cost and slow-turn nature of service inventory make precision essential. Overstocking can trap millions in idle parts, while understocking risks SLA penalties, customer dissatisfaction, and operational disruptions. Adding complexity are reverse logistics flows, which must be tightly integrated into planning to avoid unnecessary new part purchases and maximize repair yield.

5. **Impact of Product Entitlements of SPSCM** – Inventory planning must also account for whether a customer is under warranty, has a service contract, or is out-of-coverage. These entitlements change over time and often influence service priority, replacement policy, and part availability. In highly regulated and high-uptime industries, such as semiconductor equipment manufacturing, aligning inventory availability to dynamic entitlements becomes a critical—and costly—balancing act.

Understanding these five challenges isn't just helpful—it is foundational. Each one influences the other and requires a coordinated strategy across systems, processes, and people. The chapters ahead explore each in detail, unpacking their root causes, operational implications, and real-world use cases to provide a practical framework for mastering SPSCM in today's increasingly complex landscape.

Chapter 7

Challenge #1:
Diversity of Service Models

Chapter Overview

Service Parts Supply Chain Management (SPSCM) is not a one-size-fits-all discipline; it spans a variety of operational models that reflect the diverse ways in which organizations deliver maintenance, repair, and support services across industries. Among the most prominent are **Maintenance, Repair and Overhaul (MRO)**, **OEM Field Repair and Maintenance**, **Centralized Repair**, and **Service-Only Provider** models. Each of these represents a distinct approach to managing service parts and labor, shaped by factors such as product complexity, customer location, asset criticality, and service agreements. Understanding these foundational models is essential to designing and operating an effective SPSCM strategy tailored to the specific demands of a company's product and service landscape.

Before jumping into the different SPSCM model types, it is important that we circle back to the type of products that a company manufactures as this will help to delineate the MRO model from the OEM field repair and maintenance model. This starts with defining what is a consumable and non-consumable product.

Defining Product Types –
Consumables and Non-Consumables

Every company operates a supply chain, whether it involves tangible products, software delivery, or purely service-based operations. Tangible product supply chains can be categorized into two main types: **consumable and non-consumable products**.

- **Consumable products** are used up or disposed of after use. Examples include paper towels, clothing, packaged food, and disposable items like earbuds.

- **Non-consumable products** are durable items that are not consumed upon use and may require maintenance or service throughout their lifespan. Examples include aircraft, MRI machines, and consumer electronics.

Tangible Product Supply Chains	Examples	Lifecycle
Consumables	Paper towels, clothing, sport equipment, disposable ear buds, grocery items	Short
Non-Consumables	Consumer electronics, capital equipment (MRI, heavy machinery), refrigerators, airplanes	Short to Long Term

Regardless of the type of products—consumable or non-consumable—a company manufactures, every organization operates a forward supply chain to deliver products to customers. In parallel, each manufacturing facility requires a version of a SPSC and a supporting SPSCM function to meet internal maintenance needs of the factory itself—a model known as **MRO**.

For manufacturers of **non-consumable products**, there is often an additional, externally focused SPSC and SPSCM function dedicated to support the post-sale product repair and maintenance in the field. This is commonly referred to as **OEM Field Repair and Maintenance**.

Another common externally focused non-consumable model is **Centralized Repair**, where products are shipped to a designated repair center rather than being repaired on-site. This model is especially prevalent in industries such as electronics, telecommunications, and aerospace, where equipment can be modular and economically shipped for off-site diagnostics and repair. In this approach, SPSCM must be tightly integrated with logistics and triage operations to manage inbound parts flows, turnaround times, and repair capacity. Centralized repair models introduce unique supply chain challenges, such as managing repair loop inventory, coordinating with third-party repair vendors, and forecasting repairable part returns. While they offer scale efficiencies and cost control, they also require precise planning to avoid service delays and ensure customer satisfaction.

In addition, some companies specialize in SPSCM without manufacturing any product themselves. These **Service-Only Providers** focus on delivering parts and labor to support a wide range of products across industries or within a specific product type.

SPSCM Type	
MRO	Internally focused in support of manufacturing facility

SPSCM Type	
OEM Field Repair & Maintenance	Externally focused in support of field repair and maintenance by the product manufacturer or its affiliate at the customer location
Centralized Repair	Externally focused but defective products are shipped to a centralized facility for repair or maintenance
Service-Only Providers	Externally focused service only providers that support a range of other OEM products in the field

Internally Focused SPSCM – MRO (Maintenance, Repair, and Operations)

The **Maintenance, Repair, and Operations** (**MRO**) within a manufacturing company is responsible for managing spares parts and supplies necessary to maintain and repair machinery, equipment, and factory infrastructure. Just as each product manufacturer has a forward supply chain, they will also have an MRO function to sustain the factory where those products are produced.

For a **consumable manufacturer** like Procter & Gamble or a **non-consumable manufacturer** like Boeing, each will have an MRO supply chain supporting a wide range of material, including necessary service parts and equipment required for factory operations.

This inventory managed by MRO is distinct from the raw materials and components used in product manufacturing. The procurement, storage, and distribution of these spare parts are managed through a dedicated SPSCM function **within the framework of FSCM**. In essence, the MRO is a service parts supply chain that is internally owned and managed by the manufacturer to support ongoing production operations.

The Role of MRO in a Manufacturing Environment

Within a factory, various types of heavy machinery and support systems are required to manufacture products. These complex systems and machinery, often referred to as capital equipment, exist in different stages in their lifecycle.

In most manufacturing environments, a combination of **Original Equipment Manufacturers (OEM)** supported and internally maintained equipment exists:

- Some machinery is covered under OEM warranties and service agreements, meaning the MRO relies on the OEM's service parts supply chain for maintenance and repairs.
- The remaining equipment is maintained internally by the company's own MRO service parts supply chain and repair technicians.

MRO (Maintenance, Repair & Operations)

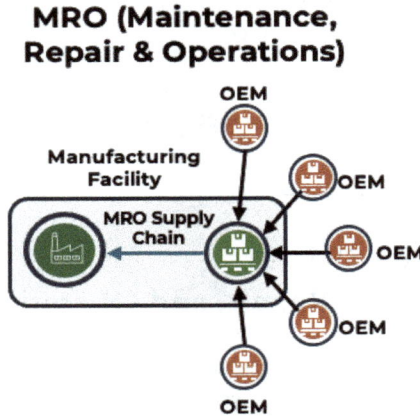

For equipment and products no longer covered under OEM warranties or service agreements, the internal MRO team performs maintenance and service activities. This requires an internal service parts supply chain to:

- Plan, forecast, purchase, and store service parts for scheduled maintenance activities. Examples include O-rings, screws, fittings, sensors, lightbulbs, filters, and lubricants.
- Maintain on-site inventory to address unexpected equipment failures, ensuring smooth manufacturing operations with minimal disruptions.

Each manufacturing facility within the company's forward supply chain maintains its own MRO supply chain operation, as service parts are stored on-site for quick response times. However, a centralized MRO supply chain management team often oversees shared functions such as:

- Planning and forecasting
- Purchasing and supplier management
- Inventory optimization across multiple factory locations

MRO supply chains rely on common suppliers to replenish safety stock, ensuring operational continuity. For high-value, infrequently failing service parts, the MRO supply chain may depend on OEMs or third-party suppliers for on-demand replacements during unexpected failures.

Unique Challenges with MRO

MRO SPSCM presents a unique and complex set of challenges due to its internal operational focus. Unlike customer-facing supply chains that support external product users, MRO supports the performance and uptime of a company's own production assets—such as manufacturing equipment, infrastructure, and capital-intensive machinery. Because these assets are central to operational continuity, any delay in part availability can result in significant downtime, lost productivity, and increased maintenance costs. This drives a critical need for high service levels, even for rarely used, expensive parts.

One of the major challenges in MRO SPSCM is balancing availability with costs. Companies must decide how much inventory to carry for parts that may be used infrequently but are essential when needed. These "just-in-case" inventory requirements can strain budgets and storage capacity, especially for low-turn, high-cost items. Unlike FSCs, where demand is often more predictable, MRO demand is driven by unplanned maintenance events and failure patterns that are difficult to forecast.

Another core issue is data fragmentation and lack of visibility. MRO environments often operate using outdated or siloed systems for asset tracking, maintenance planning, and parts procurement. This lack of integration between supply chain and maintenance systems impairs the ability to forecast demand, track part usage history, and optimize procurement strategies. Inaccurate or incomplete data on installed base components, maintenance history, and part interchangeability further complicates inventory decisions.

Additionally, long lead times for specialized, obsolete, or vendor-managed parts pose a significant risk. MRO supply chains may need to source from limited suppliers, sometimes requiring long-term relationships to ensure continuity. In industries with older equipment or long asset lifespans—such as aerospace, utilities, or heavy manufacturing—parts may no longer be commercially available, requiring repair, refurbishment, or reverse engineering as part of the supply strategy.

To address these challenges, best-in-class MRO supply chains align closely with maintenance operations, use advanced analytics and failure prediction, develop strong supplier networks, and invest in technologies that improve visibility across systems. Strategic stocking, supplier agreements, and lifecycle planning become essential to managing cost and risk effectively.

Challenge Area	Description
Downtime Sensitivity	Unavailable parts can halt operations, leading to high cost and production loss.
Unpredictable Demand	Driven by equipment failures and maintenance schedules—hard to forecast accurately
Inventory Cost vs. Availability	Need to stock expensive, slow-moving parts for contingency, increasing holding costs
Data Silos and Invisibility	Disconnected systems limit tracking of parts usage, maintenance history, or special sourcing.
Obsolete/Specialized Parts	Long lead times or discontinued parts requiring repair, refurbishment, or special sourcing
System Integration	Limited integration between procurement, maintenance, and asset management impairs planning.
Supplier Dependency	Reliance on niche or OEM suppliers can introduce delays and increase costs.

Use Case:
MRO SPSCM Challenges in Semiconductor Manufacturing

In the semiconductor industry, factories—commonly referred to as "fabs"—operate highly complex and capital-intensive equipment such as photolithography scanners, ion implanters, etchers, and chemical vapor deposition (CVD) systems. These machines are critical to maintaining the precise, uninterrupted workflows required to produce silicon wafer-based computer chips, and any disruption in their function can result in immediate production losses that cost millions of dollars per day.

The MRO supply chain within a fab is responsible for ensuring the constant availability of spare parts and consumables needed for both scheduled maintenance and unexpected breakdowns. However, this task is complicated by several key factors. First, many of the machines used in semiconductor production are custom-built or highly specialized, making their spare parts unique and often only available from a single OEM. For example, a lithography machine from ASML may require proprietary lenses or control modules that are not interchangeable and have long lead times. If the part is not stocked locally, even a minor failure can shut down a production line for days.

Second, semiconductors fabs typically operate 24/7 in cleanroom environments where downtime is not only expensive but highly disruptive to product integrity. The MRO team must stock a large number of low-turn, high-cost parts such as sensors, vacuum seals, power supplies, and circuit boards across a wide range of OEM products—many of which may not be used for months but must be immediately available when needed. These just-in-case stocking strategies create high carrying costs and consume valuable on-site storage space.

Third, predictive maintenance in fabs is data-intensive, but MRO SPSCM systems often lack integration with real-time asset health data. Maintenance teams may use one system for managing work orders and tracking downtime events, while supply chain teams rely on separate ERP or procurement platforms. This fragmentation leads to inefficiencies in forecasting part demand, recognizing wear-out patterns, and aligning procurement strategies with actual equipment condition.

Finally, due to the long equipment lifecycles in semiconductor fabs—some machines remain operational for ten to twenty years—the MRO supply chain must contend with obsolete parts. In many cases, the OEM may no longer support certain systems, requiring the fab to engage third-party suppliers, reverse engineering services, or refurbishment partners to sustain operations.

In the high-stakes environment, effective MRO SPSCM is not just a cost center—it is a strategic enabler of uptime, throughput, and yield. Companies that invest in predictive analytics, integrated maintenance and supply chain systems, and collaborative supplier relationships are better equipped to mitigate risks and ensure manufacturing continuity.

Externally Focused SPSCM Operation

Non-consumable manufacturers are considered **Original Equipment Manufacturer (OEM)** of the products they sell. Once a product leaves the factory, OEMs must support additional customer-facing service parts supply chain models beyond their own internal MRO activities. These support requirements include warranty service and maintenance, service agreement repairs, and transactional service part orders, all of which necessitate an externally focused SPSCM operation.

Within externally focused SPSCM, three primary models are commonly found:

- **Field Repair and Maintenance** – The OEM repairs or maintains the product at the client's location.
- **Centralized Repair** – The OEM repairs or refurbishes defective products at a designated repair facility after receiving them from the customer.
- **Service Only Providers** – These are independent service providers (not OEMs) that maintain and repair products from multiple OEMs, typically within a specific product vertical.

OEM Field Repair and Maintenance SPSCM

The **OEM Field Repair and Maintenance model** is among the most sophisticated and demanding structures within SPSCM. Unlike the MRO, this model must support reactive, location-specific, and equipment-sensitive demand across a globally distributed customer base. OEMs not only manufacture and deliver capital equipment, but also retain responsibility for maintaining and servicing that equipment in the field—either through their own service technicians or authorized partners.

Even when supporting a limited product portfolio—one they intimately understand—OEMs face extraordinary complexity. Their service operations must respond to both proactive (scheduled maintenance, upgrades) and reactive (break-fix) demand. This dual path is further complicated by the multi-echelon network infrastructure required to fulfill parts orders quickly and cost-effectively across a wide geography. The multi-tier nature of the OEM service network—consisting of central warehouses, regional depots, and forward-stocking locations—is a unique challenge and is discussed separately in a later chapter.

When a customer experiences a failure or requests maintenance, the OEM dispatches a trained technician to the site. This technician is responsible for diagnosing the issue and performing the necessary repairs. The service parts required for these repairs are pulled from strategically positioned inventories, often located near high concentrations of installed base to enable fast response and SLA compliance.

OEM
Field Repair & Maintenance

The OEM's SPSCM organization plays a central role in enabling this responsiveness. It is responsible for:

- Forecasting and planning part needs for installation, warranty services, service contract, and ad-hoc calls
- Managing inventories across multiple levels of the supply network—global hubs, regional distribution centers, and forward-stocking locations (FSLs)
- Coordinating the service of both field technicians and customer-managed repairs
- Supporting a broad array of customers across various industries and global locations
- Meeting strict Service Level Agreements (SLAs) that often demand same-day or next-day part availability and technician dispatch

For OEM's selling capital-intensive equipment—such as semiconductor lithography machines, medical devices, or industrial robotics—the post-sale commitment is significant. Clients typically operate under long-term warranties and service agreements, during which time the OEM is fully responsible for uptime. To fulfill these obligations, the OEM maintains a dedicated service parts inventory distinct from any inventory managed by the client's internal MRO team. This separation ensures OEM technicians can access the right parts under the right service conditions without conflicting with customer-owned inventories.

Adding further complexity, the OEM's SPSCM must serve two parallel demand streams:

1. **Internal field technicians** conducting warranty repairs, upgrades, or repair and preventive maintenance under service contracts

2. **Customer-managed MRO teams** ordering parts for self-directed maintenance and repairs after the warranty or contract expires

This dual service obligation creates unique inventory management, demand planning, and fulfillment challenges, particularly when both streams require the same part types at unpredictable intervals.

Use Case:
ASML's Dual-Path SPSCM Model
in the Semiconductor Industry

ASML, a leading Dutch manufacturer of photolithography systems for the semiconductor industry, exemplifies the complexity of the OEM Field Repair and Maintenance model. ASML's machines are among the most advanced and capital-intensive in the world, with single units costing upwards of $150 million. These machines are mission-critical to chip manufacturers like TSMC, Intel, and Samsung, who cannot afford unplanned downtime.

To support its global installed base, ASML maintains a multi-echelon service parts network composed of central warehouses in the Netherlands and the U.S., regional hubs in Asia and Europe, and dozens of forward-stocking location near major chip fabs. This network enables rapid parts delivery to customer sites across the globe, often within hours.

ASML's SPSCM faces the dual challenge of:

- Supplying its own field service engineers to perform complex repairs and upgrades on-site, often under strict uptime guarantees
- Fulfilling parts request from customer—like TSMC or Intel—who perform their own maintenance using internal MRO teams, especially after warranty periods expire

For example, TSMC may have several ASML machines on-site—some under active service contracts and others managed internally. In a given week, ASML might ship parts to:

- Its own service engineers performing a scheduled laser upgrade on a machine under contract
- TSMC's MRO team replacing a failed actuator on a legacy unit outside the service agreement

To further complicate matters, ASML must manage entitlement data to ensure correct billing and part sourcing. If a part is consumed under warranty, it is covered under contract. If the same part is ordered by TSMC's MRO team, it

---

is treated as a commercial sale. This distinction affects inventory classification, financial reporting, and customer service protocols. There is also a challenge in recognition of a true part failure at TSMC. TSMC's MRO might be ordering the part because it increased its on-hand inventory for a part, not a part failure. This makes it a challenge for the ASML SPSCM to forecast based on actual part failure demand. This will be discussed in a later chapter on true demand recognition.

ASML's experience illustrates how the OEM Field Repair Maintenance model requires an integrated SPSCM strategy that supports:

- SLA-driven responsiveness for field engineers
- Seamless coordination with customer-owned MRO supply chains
- Real-time inventory visibility across multiple echelons
- Strong forecasting, entitlements management, and reverse logistics capabilities

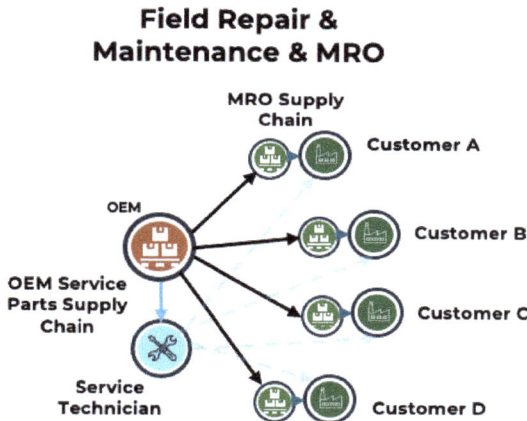

Field Repair & Maintenance & MRO

Key Challenges in the OEM Field Repair and Maintenance Model

Challenge Area	Description
Dual Demand Streams	Must support both internal field technicians (under warranty/service contracts) and external

Challenge Area	Description
	customer MRO (post-contract), often requiring the same parts
Multi-Echelon Inventory Network	Requires a distributed network of global, regional, and local stocking locations to meet aggressive SLAs
Forecasting Complexity	Demand is driven by unpredictable failures, service contracts, and customer self-maintenance activities; accurate forecasting must account for both streams
Entitlement & Contract Management	Must distinguish between contract-covered service and commercial part sales to ensure proper billing, inventory allocation, and SLA adherence
Inventory Segmentation	Needs separate inventory pools for service contract support versus customer-directed purchases, increasing complexity and cost
Installed Base Visibility	Accurate data on equipment location, configuration, and service status is essential for planning and dispatch.
Response Time Pressure	SLAs may require same-day or next-day delivery of critical parts.

Centralized Repair

Some OEMs design products and service strategies around the concept of centralized repair, where defective or failed equipment is shipped back to a dedicated facility for service rather than being fixed in the field. This model is especially effective for mobile or modular products that are not deeply embedded in customer infrastructure. Industries such as consumer electronics, medical devices, and automotive components often adopt this approach due to the economies of scale and control it offers.

In a centralized repair model, the OEM—or a designated third-party provider— operates one or more specialized repair facilities where skilled technicians and the full range of service parts are co-located. Customers send in failed products, and repairs are completed under warranty or as a paid service. By centralizing labor, diagnostics, and inventory, OEMs reduce the complexity of servicing products in the field and improve quality control. Additionally, this model allows for greater efficiency and standardization, often leveraging remanufacturing and part reclamation processes to reduce costs.

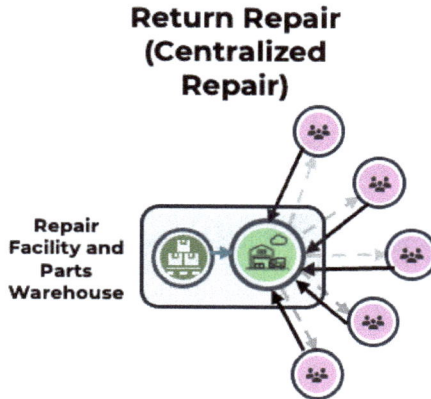

Return Repair (Centralized Repair)

Repair Facility and Parts Warehouse

Some centralized repair facilities further streamline operations by offering an **advanced exchange program**: customers receive a refurbished replacement unit immediately, while their defective unit is later repaired and restocked. This minimizes customer downtime while maintaining efficient throughput in the repair facility.

Use Case:
Centralized Repair for Semiconductor Test Equipment

In the semiconductor industry, test and measurement equipment such as parametric testers, probe stations, or spectrum analyzers can cost hundreds of thousands of dollars and are essential to maintaining yield and quality in chip fabrication. One leading OEM of such equipment operates a centralized repair facility in the U.S. to handle returns of these complex systems.

When a system in the field fails, the customer logs a support case, and the OEM initiates a controlled return process. The defective system or module is de-installed and shipped back to the central repair facility. There, a team of highly trained technicians, with access to proprietary diagnostics and all required service parts, perform detailed root cause analysis, repairs, refurbishes, and validates it to original specifications.

The OEM maintains a buffer inventory of refurbished subsystems to support rapid exchange programs for high-priority customers. Given the size and complexity of the equipment, field service is often impractical and too costly.

Additionally, central repair allows the OEM to reclaim parts, perform engineering upgrades during service, and maintain full traceability across serialized components. However, this model requires tight coordination between the customer, logistics providers, repair operations, and the centralized service parts supply chain.

Centralized Repair SPSCM Challenges

Challenge Area	Description
Long Turnaround Times (TAT)	Shipment to and from centralized repair adds lead time, which must be mitigated through exchanges and rapid processing.
Reverse Logistics	Requires efficient and traceable processes for customer returns, inbound inspections, and repair triage
Refurbishment and Reuse	Managing parts harvesting from returned products and integrating them into the supply chain adds complexity.
Capacity and Scheduling	Repair centers must balance fluctuating workloads with technician availability and parts inventory.
Inventory Planning	Requires forecasting of parts needed for repairs as well as buffer inventory for advanced exchange programs
Cost Allocation	Determining warranty versus non-warranty repair costs, refurbish economics, and return credits can be complex.

Service-Only Provider (SOP) Model

The **Service-Only Provider (SOP)** model is built around delivering maintenance, repair, and operational support services without manufacturing the equipment being serviced. These companies are solely focused on ensuring uptime and functionality of customer equipment, often supporting multiple OEM brands. While the concept of service-only organizations is common in industries like healthcare (e.g., doctor's offices), professional service (e.g., consulting or accounting firms), there is another specialized category of SOPs exists—technical service providers that maintain and repair physical assets and complex systems across industries.

Examples of Technical SOPs

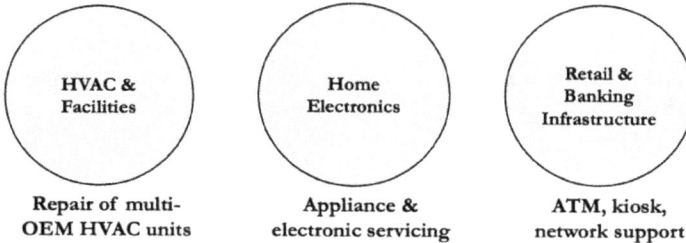

HVAC & Facilities	Home Electronics	Retail & Banking Infrastructure
Repair of multi-OEM HVAC units	Appliance & electronic servicing	ATM, kiosk, network support

These SOPs fill a critical niche in modern service ecosystems, especially as OEMs outsource field service operations to external partners for cost, scale, or regional coverage reasons.

How Service-Only Providers Operate

SOPs maintain a combination of field technicians and a specialized SPSCM function to enable efficient, rapid, and geographically distributed repairs. Unlike OEMs, they are not constrained by brand boundaries; their value lies in technical versatility, responsiveness, and cost-efficiency.

Technicians in this model are often equipped with service vehicles stocked with essential multi-brand parts, allowing them to resolve issues on a first visit. Centralized depots and regional distribution centers replenish these mobile inventories and support non-standard part delivery for scheduled or reactive repairs.

To succeed, SOPs must:

- Understand multiple OEM systems and failure profiles
- Build demand forecasts without direct access to OEM design or failure data
- Maintain a lean, highly responsive supply chain that can pivot based on customer priorities and equipment criticality

Use Case:
SOP in the Semiconductor Industry –
Third-Party Cleanroom Equipment Maintenance

In semiconductor fabrication, cleanroom environments house critical tools such as wafer inspection systems, chemical wet benches, and environmental control units. These tools often come from different OEMs and require specialized knowledge and components for ongoing service.

A third-party Service-Only Provider that operates in this space offers full maintenance support for these systems. Semiconductor manufacturers contract these providers to manage all equipment service within their cleanroom facilities—especially for tools that are out of warranty or no longer supported by OEMs.

The SOP is responsible for:

- Maintaining **multi-brand service parts inventory**, including rare or obsolete components
- **Deploying specialized technicians** trained across several OEM platforms
- **Coordinating spare parts logistics** with high-sensitivity cleanroom environments
- Managing **preventative maintenance schedules,** urgent failures, and part refurbishments

This model allows fabs to extend the life of the equipment, reduce reliance on multiple OEM service contracts, and consolidate maintenance under a single, performance-based SLA.

Service-Only Providers SPSCM Challenges

Challenge Area	Description
Multi-OEM Parts Sourcing	SOPs must procure service parts for a wide range of OEM products, often with limited direct access to OEM supply chains.
Forecasting Without OEM Data	Lack of visibility in OEM design and failure data complicates predictive maintenance and inventory planning.

Challenge Area	Description
Mobile Inventory Management	Vehicle-stored parts must be tracked, replenished, and balanced across large geographies.
Reverse Logistics for Defective Parts	Collecting and routing failed parts for repair, reuse, or core credit adds logistical complexity.
Client-Specific Customization	SOPs often support custom equipment configurations or localized modifications, requiring specialized parts stocking.
Warranty versus Non-Warranty Work	Must distinguish parts and labor across OEM-sponsored, customer paid, or internal contract services

Operating Multiple Supply Chain Models Simultaneously

To conclude the discussion on SPSCM model types, it is critical to recognize that most non-consumable product companies operate **multiple, overlapping supply chain models** at the same time. These models are not mutually exclusive—they are tailored to the function and service demands that arise across the product lifecycle. Each model has unique characteristics in terms of inventory positioning, lead time expectations, technician enablement, and customer touchpoints.

For example, ASML offers a compelling example of a company operating multiple SPSCM models simultaneously to support its highly complex and mission-critical products.

ASML's SPSCM Models:

Model Type	Application within ASML
Forward Supply Chain (FSC)	Manages sourcing and production of thousands of precision components required for lithography machines
MRO Service Parts Supply Chain	Maintains ASML's own production and cleanroom tools, including metrology and inspection equipment

Model Type	Application within ASML
OEM Field Repair and Maintenance	Supports customers like TSMC, Intel, and Samsung with on-site field technicians and rapid spare parts delivery
Centralized Repair	Operates specialized global repair centers where failed modules or subassemblies are sent for diagnostic testing, repair, and requalification
Service-Only Provider Partnerships	In some regions, partners with third-party providers for less critical maintenance, using ASML-certified parts and procedures

How These Models Interact

A single ASML customer site may simultaneously trigger activity across multiple supply chains:

- When a critical module fails, ASML dispatches a field engineer supported by a regional parts depot **(OEM Field Repair)**.
- The defective module is returned to a centralized repair facility in Europe or Asia for diagnostic and rework **(Centralized Repair)**.
- The same customer may also procure preventative maintenance kits directly from ASML to be used by their own engineers **(Customer MRO versus OEM supply)**.
- Meanwhile, ASML's internal cleanroom operations rely on their **own MRO supply chain** to ensure calibration, test equipment, and cleanroom tools remain functional and in spec.

Disclaimer: The ASML examples provided are intended for illustrative purposes only and does not represent actual details of ASML's service part supply chain models, operations, or performance. It is a hypothetical use case created to demonstrate how multiple SPSCM models might coexist within a complex OEM environment.

Closing Summary

Understanding the various SPSCM models—MRO, OEM Field Repair and Maintenance, Centralized Repair, and Service-Only Providers—is critical to grasping the full complexity of modern after-sale support environments. Each model addresses unique operational contexts, asset types, and service delivery strategies, and often coexist within the same enterprise to meet diverse business needs. From internally focused MRO supply chains sustaining production uptime, to externally focused OEM networks supporting global installed bases, to centralized repair hubs optimizing return logistics, and third-party service providers managing multi-brand service ecosystems—each model requires distinct planning, inventory, and execution approaches. Recognizing and designing supply chains tailored to each of these models is essential for achieving both cost efficiency and service excellence in today's asset-intensive industries.

Chapter 8
Challenge #2: Dynamics of SPSCM Demand Forecasting

Introduction

As highlighted in Chapter 2, one of the fundamental differences between FSCM and SPSCM is the nature of their demand sources. In FSCM, demand is driven by sales forecasts and customer orders for a product, making forecasting more predictable and limited to a smaller set of actively sold items.

In contrast, SPSCM's demand arises when a service part—one of potentially thousands—is ordered to address an event involving products still in active sales or legacy products in use that still require support. This makes SPSCM forecasting more complex, as the trigger for demand can be highly unpredictable at the individual part level.

Peeling back the layers of service parts demand reveals several dynamics that are essential to effectively forecast. These interdependent factors significantly increase planning complexity, often leading to inflated inventories, poor inventory turns, and challenges in meeting customer expectations.

In this chapter we will examine the critical influences that shape SPSCM demand and how each must be considered for more accurate forecasting. This chapter examines:

1. **Part Failure Rate Prediction and Variability**
2. **Product Installed Base Visibility and Lifecycle Stage – The Second Critical Driver of the Demand Equation**
3. **Preventative Maintenance Parts – The Third Element in the Demand Equation**
4. **Installed Base Entitlement Coverage – The Fourth Contributor to SPSCM Dynamic Demand**

Taken together, these four dimensions must be integrated into forecasting strategies to maximize accuracy.

To start, it's important to establish a baseline understanding of "true demand" in SPSCM. **True demand** refers to the actual service parts usage that results from a failure or scheduled maintenance event. It is distinct from the demand reflected in ERP, planning, or inventory systems based on parts shipments. At its core, if SPSCM planners cannot forecast based on true demand, any planning effort will be suboptimal.

Part Failure Rate Prediction and Variability

Understanding the variability and nature of part failure rates is essential for effective SPSCM. Before examining their impact, it's important to distinguish between two related concepts: *service event failures* and *service parts failures*. Clarifying this distinction helps SPSCM professionals forecast demand accurately and allocate inventory effectively.

Service Event Failure Rates versus Service Parts Failure Rates

When a product fails, it initiates a service event—such as a support call, diagnosis, or repair. These events are measured using key reliability metrics, including:

Reliability Metric	Description
Mean Time Between Failures (MTBF)	Indicates how often a product fails; a core reliability indicator
Mean Time to Repair (MTTR)	Measures the average time needed to diagnose and resolve an issue, influenced by design, technician skill, and part availability
Mean Time Between Planned Maintenance (MTBPM)	Reflects scheduled service intervals, such as a 36,000-mile car service

Field service teams use these metrics to plan coverage and track performance. However, not all service events require parts. Thus, for the SPSCM planners, the product MTBF is relevant, but the actual trigger for parts demand is part-level failure.

Product quality and reliability directly influence service parts demand. If a product never failed, SPSCM would only focus on preventative maintenance and consumables which are easier to predict. Instead, unexpected failures—especially during product ramp-up stages when real-world failure rates exceed design estimates—creates planning risks. With supplier lead times of sixty to ninety days or more, stockouts are inevitable without accurate forecasting.

In industries like semiconductor equipment manufacturing, uptime commitments often exceed 95%, allowing little tolerance for unplanned downtime. This downtime must account for:

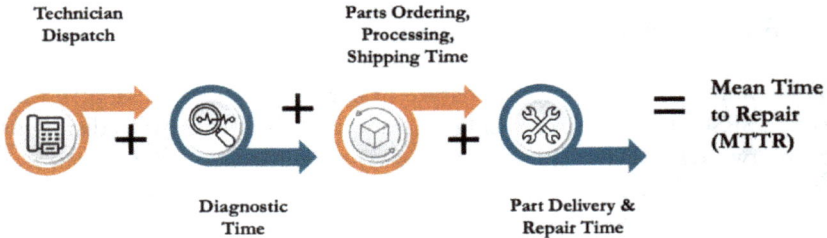

When product MTBF is low—fails frequently—even slight delays in parts availability can jeopardize service level agreements.

Service Parts Failure Rates

SPSCM forecasting extends beyond product-level failures to predict part-specific failure rates. The **service part failure rate** is a measurement of the likelihood and frequency of a component replacement need.

Each service part has a unique failure behavior and must be treated as an independent planning entity. Parts often span multiple product platforms, further complicating forecasts. Thus, SPSCM requires a more granular approach than product-level MTBF alone.

Why Failure Rates Matter in SPSCM

Failure rate metrics enable:

- **Granular forecasting**: Predicting when and how individual parts will fail
- **Lifecycle-aware planning**: Accounting for infant mortality and wear-out stages common in a part's life

Planners typically assign failure rates to parts based on:

- Historical field data for similar parts
- Engineering reliability estimates
- Manufacturer-supplied data

As field data accumulates, historical usage is incorporated into forecasts, particularly for stable, high-usage parts. However, low-volume, erratic parts often depend on estimates, increasing uncertainty.

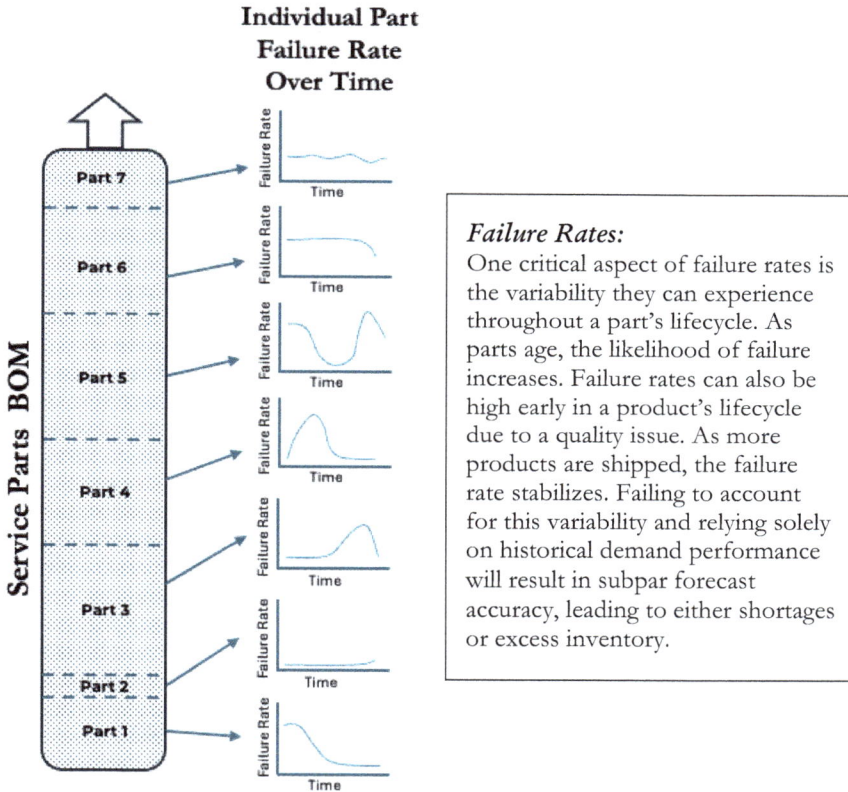

Individual Part Failure Rate Over Time

> *Failure Rates:*
> One critical aspect of failure rates is the variability they can experience throughout a part's lifecycle. As parts age, the likelihood of failure increases. Failure rates can also be high early in a product's lifecycle due to a quality issue. As more products are shipped, the failure rate stabilizes. Failing to account for this variability and relying solely on historical demand performance will result in subpar forecast accuracy, leading to either shortages or excess inventory.

Forecasting failure rates across a global installed base introduces considerable complexity:

Challenges	Complexity
High serviceable part counts	Hundreds of parts per product
Lifecycle variance	Failure rates vary based on product maturity
Seasonality	Environmental factors can skew failure patterns

Challenges	Complexity
Geographic variance	Climate and local infrastructure affect wear
User behavior	Varies significantly by application and operator

Effective forecasting requires continuous adjustment. Planning software helps, but robust historical data is essential. Human oversight remains critical in interpreting anomalies and adjusting plans accordingly.

Managing Failure Rate Variability

Every service part undergoes its own lifecycle as the product ages. Beyond age and wear, other factors drive service parts demand, including:

- Installation mistakes
- Missing or defective components
- Shipping damage
- Customer MRO inventory replenishment

During early product life, these factors distort early demand signals. Mistaking them for true failures risks overstocking and later obsolescence.

Aging Parts

Older parts are more likely to fail. Forecasting systems often weigh recent usage more heavily to reflect this, and spikes in demand are common near the end of warranty periods. However, most systems are backward-looking and struggle to forecast such events proactively.

Advanced SPSCM operations leverage telemetry and predictive monitoring, but most organizations lack this infrastructure. Stockouts and escalations remain prevalent.

Seasonal and Environmental Effects

Environmental conditions heavily influence reliability. For example:

- **High heat and sand infiltration** in the Middle East caused unexpected laptop fan and heatsink failures.
- **Harsh winters accelerated rust and corrosion** in northern climates.

Laptop Heatsinks Service Parts Failure Rate

Location	Installed Base	Failure Rate	Seasonality
United States	1,000	5%	No
Norway	1,000	3%	No
Saudi Arabia	1,000	12%	Yes
India	1,000	10%	Yes
Singapore	1,000	7%	No

Unpredictable user behavior can also skew demand. For instance, a viral mobile app once encouraged users to toss phones in the air—leading to a surge in screen replacements. Such trends are nearly impossible to predict but must be identified and addressed.

First-Hand Challenges in Semiconductor Manufacturing; A Use Case in MTBF and Service Parts Failure Dynamics

From my time as a field engineer supporting global semiconductor fabs, equipment uptime was paramount. Even brief unplanned downtime could disrupt production schedules and cost millions in lost wafer yield.

Take, for example, a plasma etcher, with a tool-level Mean Time Between Failure (MTBF) of 5,000 hours. That metric suggests system failure might occur roughly every seven months. While that appears reliable from the OEM perspective, it doesn't reflect service parts dynamics.

Most parts replacements do not stem from full system outages. Instead, they occur due to wear, contamination, or marginal degradation. Preventative swaps and diagnostic replacements are common, often involving multiple parts shipped for one repair event—only one of which may be used. The others are returned or scrapped, but their initial demand affected planning and availability.

The etcher may meet its MTBF target but disconnects remain, including:

- Individual components, such as RF generators, endpoint sensors, or valves, may each have their own failure or replacement intervals—some as short as 500 or 1,000 hours.

- In the absence of a system-wide failure, parts are regularly replaced due to wear, contamination, tolerance drift, or as a precautionary measure.

For example, during a routine process deviation investigation, I might overnight three parts—suspecting any of them could be the cause. Even though only one would be used, all three impacted planning and availability in the service parts supply chain. The remaining two would be returned or repurposed, but their temporary absence from inventory affected global part availability and replenishment timelines.

Compounding this challenge, any service event labeled "urgent down" would override standard SPSCM logic. Parts were pulled from regional hubs, other customers' allocations, or even R&D labs. This triage process helped get the tool running quickly—but it caused ripple effects throughout the multi-echelon service parts network. Regular replenishment cycles were delayed, and suppliers were suddenly under pressure to support urgent resupply from multiple locations at once.

In Summary

With many semiconductor tools having hundreds of unique service parts, each with its own failure characteristics, the service parts supply chain cannot rely solely on tool-level MTBF metrics. Instead, accurate planning depends on part-specific failure rates, field history, and usage behavior—factors that often fluctuate across customers, geographies, and the product environment.

Product Installed Base Visibility and Lifecycle Stage: The Second Critical Driver of the Demand Equation

Understanding the Installed Base

The **installed base** refers to the number of product units that are currently **in active use** in the field. It is distinct from the total number of units sold, as products naturally retire as they reach the end of their useful life or are damaged beyond repair. As such, what truly matters for SPSCM is the **dynamic installed base**. This refers to the constantly changing pool of active units requiring support.

SPSCM planning has traditionally relied on historical demand to generate forecasts. While advanced forecasting algorithms can smooth out erratic usage patterns and apply trend-based weighting, these systems are inherently backward-looking. As a result, organizations often maintain liberal safety stock buffers to hedge against inaccuracies.

However, a more forward-looking approach is possible by incorporating leading indicators into the forecasting process. Two such indicators are:

1. Failure rate estimation of serviceable parts (discussed earlier)
2. The dynamic installed base and where each product unit is within its lifecycle

Installed Base as a Forecasting Enabler

The installed base provides critical insight into the potential demand for service parts. Knowing the projected failure rate of a component is only part of the picture. Planners must also understand:

- **How many units are deployed** and still in service
- **What stage of the lifecycle those units are in** (early use, mid-life, nearing retirement)

Without this visibility, forecast accuracy suffers, leading to either excess inventory or service-level shortfalls.

Two characteristics enhance the utility of installed base data for SPSCM forecasting:

1. **Visibility into the location and lifecycle stage** of each installed unit
2. **Forward-looking sales projections**, especially as the product scales or nears the end of its manufacturing lifecycle

Installed Base Visibility: The First Step

Accurate demand forecasting and inventory positioning in a multi-echelon network begins with installed base visibility. For capital equipment OEMs—such as those serving the semiconductor industry—this task is made somewhat easier by the nature of their products: tools like lithography machines or plasma etchers are stationary, high-value assets installed at fixed customer sites.

With this model, OEMs can track:

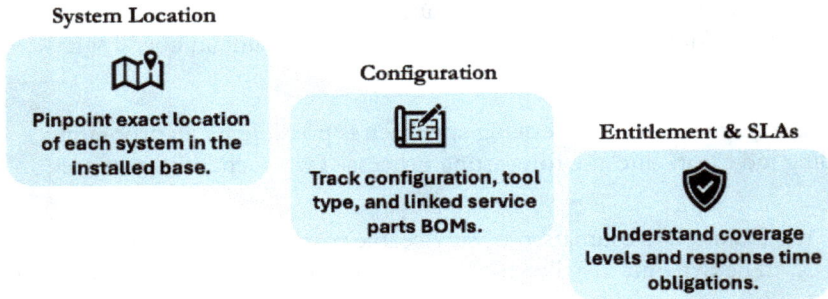

System Location

Pinpoint exact location of each system in the installed base.

Configuration

Track configuration, tool type, and linked service parts BOMs.

Entitlement & SLAs

Understand coverage levels and response time obligations.

Some industries go a step further by embedding "call home" capabilities into products. These sensors transmit usage data, alerts, diagnostic logs, and the GPS location of the product in real time—enabling automated tracking of tool performance, usage hours, and fault history. This transformation turns the installed base into a dynamic planning tool, rather than a static record.

Installed Base Lifecycle Variance: An Example

Consider a major semiconductor equipment OEM supporting a global base of plasma etching systems. Each tool includes dozens of serviceable components with varying replacement cycles.

Here's a real-world scenario:

- A fab installs 50 etchers in Year 1, with each tool sold with a 12-month standard warranty and 70% of units receiving an extended 24-month service contract.
- Over the next 24 months, another 200 units are sold globally, with similar contract distribution.
- By Year 3, the installed base peaks; early units begin to fall out of entitlement coverage.

Planners using only historical demand would observe a decline in service parts consumption and incorrectly interpret it as a drop in failure rates or usage. In reality, the demand drop is tied to the **waterfall effect** of expired entitlements, not necessarily fewer failures.

If SPSCM planning fails to incorporate installed base lifecycle visibility, the network may understock needed parts or overreact to transient demand shifts, jeopardizing uptime for still-supported units.

The Product Sales Waterfall Effect

Understanding how entitlements expire over time enables planners to anticipate how the dynamic installed base will evolve. Consider this simplified timeline:

- **Month 1**: 1,000 units are sold.
    - Of these, 500 units are standard 12-month coverage; 500 units have extended 24-month coverage.
- **Month 2**: 1,000 more units are sold with the same 500/500 service spread as in month one.
- **Month 13**: The first 500 units from month one drop out of entitlement; SPSCM obligations decline.
- **Month 25**: The remaining 500 units from month one exit support; demand continues to fall unless new units are added.

Waterfall of Service Coverage

	Month 1	Month 2	Month 13	Month 25	Month 26	Month 27
Total Products Sold	1,000	1,000				
Warranty (12 Months)	500	1000	500	500		
Extended Service (12 Months	500	1000	1000	500	500	
No Coverage			500	1000	1500	2000

Each successive sales cohort follows this pattern, creating a sales waterfall—a key forecasting input that helps identify:

- Upcoming peaks and troughs in support coverage
- When to scale service inventory up or down
- Anticipated regional demand shifts as older units retire

Without this perspective, the SPSCM model becomes reactive, responding to demand signals only after they emerge—often too late for optimized replenishment.

A subtle, often-overlooked behavior is the pre-expiration surge: customers frequently request parts replacements just before their warranties expire. This "last-minute" behavior can distort short-term demand unless planners account for entitlement expiration trends.

Installed Base Configuration: A Deeper Challenge

Many OEMs sell configurable products—common in both industrial and semiconductor equipment. While each tool may be based on common platforms, field configurations often vary:

- Optional modules are added.
- Components are upgraded or replaced during tool life.
- New product chemistries or fab requirements drive retrofit kits.

This evolving configuration landscape affects the SPBOM and, consequently, part-level forecasting. SPSCM teams must track:

- **Configuration history per unit**
- **Field upgrades** and their impact on part consumption
- **Compatibility matrices** to avoid stocking obsolete parts

Without configuration-level visibility, planners may stock incorrect parts or fail to support critical tool variants.

In Summary

For OEMs, especially those in high-stakes industries like semiconductor manufacturing, the installed base is a living dataset—not just a historical footprint. Its visibility, configuration state, and lifecycle positioning are essential to:

- Improving forecast accuracy
- Reducing stockouts and minimizing excess inventory
- Supporting proactive, lifecycle-aware planning

While it may seem obvious that installed base data should drive SPSCM processes, executing this remains a major challenge. Most organizations struggle to collect, maintain, and integrate this data across systems. This critical gap—and the data infrastructure required to close it—will be explored in detail in a later section on SPSCM data challenges.

Preventive Maintenance Parts –
The Third Element in the Demand Equation

Preventive Maintenance (PM) is the third component in the SPSCM dynamic demand equation. Unlike corrective maintenance parts, which are ordered reactively after a failure event, PM parts are associated with **planned service events**—usually aligned with manufacturing recommendations or customer-specific requirements. This planned nature allows for more predictable, time-based demand, helping stabilize otherwise erratic consumption patterns common in reactive service environments.

The ability to schedule PM activity—daily, weekly, monthly, or by runtime metrics (e.g., hours of operation, cycle count)—enables SPSCM planners to **forecast demand with a higher degree of accuracy**. Because PM parts are replaced regardless of failure, their consumption is decoupled from failure models.

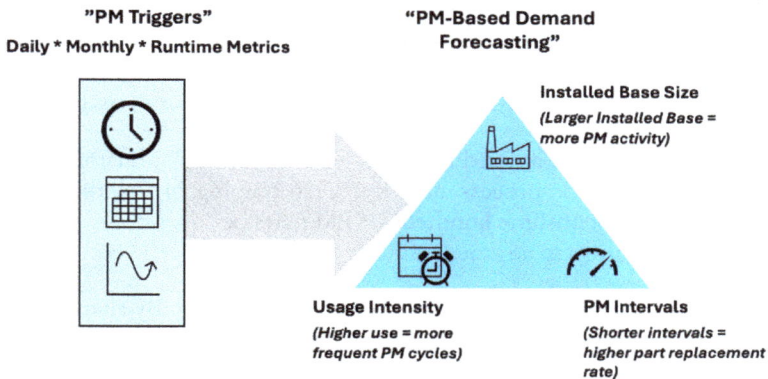

"PM Triggers"
Daily * Monthly * Runtime Metrics

"PM-Based Demand Forecasting"

Installed Base Size
(Larger Installed Base = more PM activity)

Usage Intensity
(Higher use = more frequent PM cycles)

PM Intervals
(Shorter intervals = higher part replacement rate)

This provides a leading indicator of demand, especially useful in industries with high uptime expectations and strict maintenance protocols.

Additionally, PM-driven demand allows OEMs to preposition inventory within the multi-echelon supply chain. By synchronizing service kits and part deliveries with planned maintenance schedules, planners can optimize logistics, reduce expedited shipments, and improve part availability. Moreover, packaging PM parts into standardized kits improves field technicians' efficiency and ensures correct component replacement—further supporting high service levels and cost containment.

From the SPSCM perspective, this predictability offers an opportunity to balance the reactive and proactive sides of demand. When integrated into planning models, PM parts help smooth out spikes in unplanned consumption. However, it also introduces challenges, such as ensuring customer compliance with PM schedules, managing part obsolescence when platforms are upgraded, and visibility of the installed base location, maintenance records, and runtimes.

Semiconductor Use Case: Preventive Maintenance in High-Volume Etch Tools

In the semiconductor manufacturing environment, preventive maintenance is mission-critical due to the extreme precision, cleanliness, and reliability required on the equipment. Take, for example, high-volume plasma etching systems used in advanced node fabrication. These tools operate under harsh conditions—exposing internal components to high energy plasma, chemical byproducts, and thermal cycling.

OEMs typically prescribe strict PM schedules tied to wafer counts, plasma hours, or calendar days. Common PM parts include:

- **O-rings and seals** exposed to vacuum and chemical degradation
- **Electrostatic chucks and focus rings** that experience material erosion
- **Gas line filters**, **valves**, and **lamps** that degrade from usage

These parts are replaced at fixed intervals—often monthly or quarterly. The interval depends on process intensity. A fab running 24/7 with many etch chambers may consume hundreds of PM parts per quarter—with those demands known in advance.

This creates a valuable demand signal for SPSCM planning. By aligning PM part forecasts with fab production schedules and tool runtime logs, OEMs can build highly accurate replenishment models. For instance, a PM forecast for a fab operating 25 etchers under a quarterly PM cycle would anticipate 25 times the number of each part required for that specific kit, three months in advance. These forecasts are not only more reliable but also allow OEMs to:

- Pre-build and ship PM service kits
- Minimize expedited freight due to known service windows
- Level-load procurement of consumables and high-wear items

However, failure to integrate PM parts planning into the SPSCM model can result in missed service windows, tool downtime, and even fab-wide production bottlenecks. In such a high-cost-per-hour environment, predictable PM parts demand is not just an optimization lever—it is a fundamental SPSCM requirement.

Installed Base Entitlement Coverage – The Fourth Contributor to SPSCM Dynamic Demand

A frequently overlooked yet critical dynamic in SPSCM demand forecasting is understanding entitlement coverage across the installed base. Entitlement refers to the specific level of support that an OEM is contractually obligated to provide for a given product unit in the field.

Entitlement Coverage	Description
Standard Product Warranties	Baseline coverage for defects and failures within a defined period
Extended Service Agreements	Additional paid coverage that extends support duration or scope
Uptime Guarantees	Commitments to system availability (e.g., 95% uptime monthly)
Part Delivery SLAs	Defined windows for replacement parts (e.g., four-hour, next-day delivery)

Entitlement coverage fundamentally influences **what demand the SPSCM must be ready to fulfill**—from stocking strategies across the multi-echelon network to response time requirements and part availability. Without visibility into entitlement data, planners are blind to which portion of the installed base requires guaranteed support versus those customers managing support independently. This distinction is essential for differentiating between **obligated (planned) demand and unstructured (reactive) demand**.

Entitlement and the Concept of "True Demand"

Understanding entitlement is essential for identifying true demand—the actual part consumption tied directly to product failures or scheduled maintenance activities. In SPSCM, there is rarely a clean one-to-one correlation between orders and demand. Instead, demand originates from two main streams:

- **OEM Field Service Orders** – Initiated by the OEM's technicians during warranty or contract repairs, these orders reflect actual part failures and are a reliable signal of true demand.
- **Customer MRO Orders** – Generated by customers who manage their own spare part inventories, these orders are often decoupled

from real-time failure events and, instead, follow internal planning logic, budgets, or buffer restocking cycles.

Example (for an individual product):

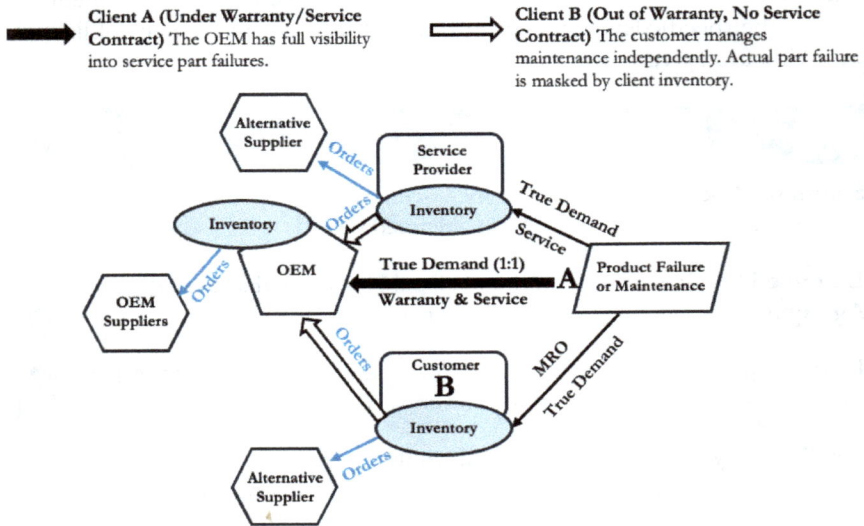

This dual-stream model complicates SPSCM forecasting because MRO-based orders do not necessarily correlate with actual failures. A customer may overstock in anticipation of failure, creating false demand signals, or understock and place last-minute orders, causing urgent spikes in demand. In either case, the OEM lacks clear insight into how parts are consumed, making it difficult to develop accurate forecasts and stock strategies.

Semiconductor Use Case: Entitlement and True Demand Visibility

In the semiconductor industry, entitlement data is vital due to the high value and operational sensitivity of capital equipment. Consider a manufacturer of **ion implanters**—a highly complex tool used in advanced semiconductor fabs. These systems are typically sold with comprehensive **two-to-five-year service contracts**, covering:

- 24/7 on-site technical support
- Predictive maintenance schedules
- Guaranteed part replacement SLAs (e.g., four-hour on-site part availability)

For entitled customers, the OEM's field service team manages all maintenance and repair, logging exact part consumption through service records. This creates a rich source of **true demand data**, enabling improved forecast accuracy for those installed units. Planners can correlate failure rate with tool usage, runtime hours, and maintenance schedules, making stocking and replenishment models more efficient.

In contrast, when service contracts expire or a customer opts out, the fab transitions to **self-managed MRO**. At this point, the OEM's visibility into consumption drops sharply. The fab may choose to maintain its own stock of high-risk parts (e.g., RF generators, power supplies, vacuum seals) based on internal usage models or budget cycles. These orders, sporadic and volume-variable, may no longer reflect real-time tool conditions or genuine part failures. The OEM sees erratic demand patterns, even if actual failure rates remain stable.

This disconnect leads to planning inefficiencies:

- **Over-forecasting**: When MRO customers build inventory for perceived risk, not real usage.
- **Under-forecasting**: When customers defer orders until parts fail, triggering urgent or emergency shipments
- **Reactive reallocation**: When unexpected MRO orders drain inventory meant for entitled customers

Without entitlement-based segmentation, the OEM might apply uniform demand logic across all installed units, ignoring contractual obligations and customer behavior patterns—leading to overstocking in some regions and critical shortages in others.

The Planning Complexity of an Evolving Entitlement Mix

The SPSCM challenge intensifies as products move through their lifecycle and the entitlement mix evolves. At product launch, nearly all units may be under warranty or covered by full-service contracts, giving the OEM full visibility. Over time, coverage expires or they transition to tiered support models. Some customers opt for service contracts, while others shift to self-managed support. New customer acquisitions and contract renewals continuously shift the entitlement landscape.

Closing Summary:
Service Parts Demand Dynamics – A Holistic View

SPSCM operates in a fundamentally different paradigm than FSCM. While FSCM benefits from a direct one-to-one relationship between product sales and demand—where each sale directly corresponds to a production or replenishment requirement—SPSCM is driven by a **multi-variable, dynamic demand equation**. This complexity arises from four interrelated drivers:

1. **Failure Rate**
2. **Preventive Maintenance (PM)**
3. **Installed Base**
4. **Entitlement Coverage**

These four dynamics are not independent; rather, they are tightly interconnected, forming a systemic model that must be understood holistically to forecast demand accurately.

The Dynamic SPSCM Demand Equation

We can summarize the core drivers of SPSCM demand with the following conceptual formula:

$$SPSCM\ Demand = f\ (Failure\ Rate\ x\ Installed\ Base) + PM\ Parts + Entitlement\ Adjustments$$

Where:

- **Failure Rate x Installed Base** estimates the core **reactive demand**—how often parts fail and how many products are out in the field that can fail.

- **PM Parts** adds **scheduled demand** that can be planned in advance, based on OEM service programs or customer PM intervals.

- **Entitlement-Driven Adjustments** reflect the **guaranteed demand** that must be fulfilled under contractual obligations (warranty, SLAs), overriding or shaping how inventory must be stocked, prioritized, and delivered.

This equation reflects how demand is shaped not just by actual parts usage, but by who owns the product, how it's maintained, and what kind of support is expected.

How Installed Base, Entitlements, and Failure Rates Interact to Shape Service Parts Demand

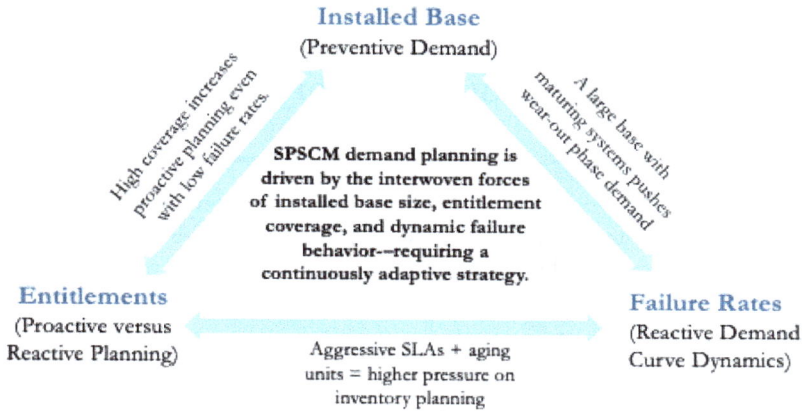

Installed Base
(Preventive Demand)

High coverage increases proactive planning even with low failure rates.

A large base with maturing systems pushes wear-out phase demand

SPSCM demand planning is driven by the interwoven forces of installed base size, entitlement coverage, and dynamic failure behavior--requiring a continuously adaptive strategy.

Entitlements
(Proactive versus
Reactive Planning)

Aggressive SLAs + aging
units = higher pressure on
inventory planning

Failure Rates
(Reactive Demand
Curve Dynamics)

- A **high installed base** with **low failure rates** can still create significant demand if preventive maintenance schedules are aggressive (e.g., semiconductor fabs replacing parts on usage cycles).
- **Entitlements** determine how much of the calculated demand must be planned proactively versus allowed to be fulfilled at lead-time or with lower priority.
- **Failure rate curves** (e.g., infant mortality, steady-state, wear-out) change over time and vary by product type and environment— affecting both PM and reactive demand.

In essence, these variables form a multidimensional **demand surface**, not a single point—one that shifts constantly based on product age, usage environment, support models, and customer behavior.

Forecasting service parts demand is **not about counting units**, but about **understanding behavior**—of machines, of customers, and of obligations. Only when failure rates, preventive maintenance, installed base, and entitlements are integrated into a unified view can SPSCM leaders move from reactive stocking to proactive, data-driven planning.

Chapter 9

Challenge #3:
The OEM Field Repair and Maintenance
Multi-Echelon Inventory Network

A defining feature of SPSCM is the need to support geographically distributed, fixed-location assets across their entire lifecycle—often under time-sensitive contractual obligations. Unlike traditional FSCM, which delivers finished goods to market, SPSCM must react to unpredictable service events in the field.

Effective execution requires not only accurate demand forecasting but also a resilient, geographically responsive inventory network. When a semiconductor tool or medical imaging system fails, every day of downtime can cost customers thousands—or even millions of dollars. To meet stringent SLAs, OEMs must build and operate multi-echelon inventory networks that ensure rapid part availability near the point of service. This complex logistical structure forms the backbone of field repair and maintenance in OEM SPSCM operations.

Field-Based Service and the Role of Multi-Echelon Networks

For many SPSCM operations, the customer base is typically global, and products are immobile, installed at client facilities. All OEMs must support an initial warranty period and, in many cases, optional long-term service contracts requiring on-site maintenance. SLAs often mandate tight response windows—such as a technician's arrival within two hours and repair completion within 24 hours—creating pressure to ensure part availability without delay.

Because stocking every part at every local location is economically infeasible, SPSCM organizations use multi-echelon inventory networks: hierarchical, regionally distributed storage systems designed to balance inventory cost and availability.

Overview: Multi-Echelon Inventory Models

SPSCM employs two fundamental inventory structures:

- **Single-Echelon Model**: Flat networks where each site manages its inventory independently

- **Multi-Echelon Model**: Hierarchical systems where centralized hubs replenish local nodes

The latter is more common in global service environments due to the diversity of products and geographic complexity.

Typical Structure:

Multi-Echelon Network

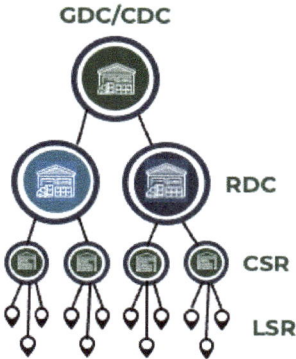

GDC/CDC

RDC

CSR

LSR

- **Global Distribution Center (GDC)**: Central hub for forecasting, procurement, and global inventory control.
- **Continental Distribution Centers (CDCs)**: Intermediate nodes serving major regional zones
- **Regional Distribution Centers (RDCs)**: Feed country-level and local nodes
- **Country Stock Rooms (CSRs)**: Buffer inventory at the national level
- **Local Stock Rooms (LSRs)**: Closest point to the customer—may include micro-warehouses, service trucks, or consignment stock

Each node holds safety stock, triggers replenishment from parent nodes, while supporting downstream service teams. Strategic stocking decisions prioritize part criticality and usage frequency to optimize capital investment.

Semiconductor Use Case:
Multi-Echelon Networks in High-Sensitivity Environments

Consider a semiconductor OEM supporting field repair for ion implanters, critical tools in chip fabrication. These machines are covered by SLAs guaranteeing uptime within a few hours of failure. A single fab may operate 24/7 in a cleanroom environment, making downtime extremely costly.

To meet service commitments, the OEM uses a tiered network:

- **Local Stock Rooms (LSRs)**: Maintain high-failure parts like RF generators and vacuum pumps near major fabs.
- **Country Stock Rooms (CSRs)**: Stock lower-use but critical parts, such as beam alignment sensors or cryogenic components

- **Regional Distribution Centers (RDCs)**: Buffer less frequently used assemblies and coordinate emergency replenishment
- **Global Distribution Center (GDC)**: Performs global forecasting and consolidates parts from multiple suppliers

For example, when a plasma source fails in a Japanese fab, the local LSR delivers the part within hours. If the part is not available locally, it is expedited from the CSR or RDC with SLA-compliant lead time. This responsiveness hinges on the network's ability to dynamically allocate inventory across tiers and regions.

Service Parts Supply Chain Inventory Network

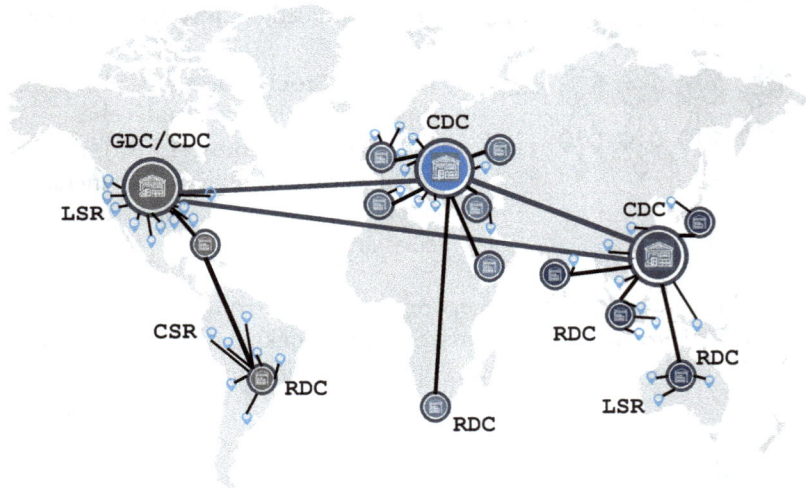

Regional Variations and Network Design Flexibility

Depending on client support requirements and regional infrastructure challenges, support from an LSR or even a CSR may not always be feasible. In some cases, clients are supported directly from an RDC instead of the lower-tier locations.

Multi-echelon designs vary based on:

- Customer concentration and SLA obligations
- Local infrastructure capabilities
- Customs and regulatory constraints

Example #1:

- **North America** – A GDC in the U.S. may directly support LSRs across the continent due to efficient transportation and harmonized trade agreements.
- **South America** – Additional tiers (e.g., CDCs) may be required to manage longer customs clearance and import processes.
- **Brazil** – Regulatory restrictions prohibit the import of repaired service parts, requiring a localized repair loop. This differs sharply from the U.S., where repaired inventory circulates freely.

Companies with global SPSCM operations face challenges such as tariffs, duties, taxes, Value Added Tax (VAT), and regulatory restrictions—all of which influence inventory movement and storage strategies. Regional organizations must navigate these varying parameters, which often differ significantly from one region to another.

Example #2:

For many SPSCM operations, utilizing repaired service parts is a key strategy to minimize new purchases, improve efficiency, and reduce service costs. However, in Brazil, the use of repaired parts is restricted to those repaired within the country—SPSCM cannot import repaired parts into Brazil.

This regulatory limitation is in contrast to North America and other parts of South America, where repaired parts can be used regardless of where they were refurbished. As a result, Brazil's restrictions necessitate a localized service parts repair network, impacting replenishment logic within the multi-echelon structure for North and South America.

Short lifecycle products, such as consumer electronics, present additional challenges due to regional variations in product specification and failure rates.

Regional challenges and regulatory variations are common across multinational product companies and business units. However, these nuances are particularly complex in SPSCM, as they directly impact the functionality and efficiency of already intricate multi-echelon inventory network.

Dynamic Demand: The Compounding Complexity Factor

What makes maintaining multi-echelon structure especially challenging is the dynamic demand equation—discussed in the last chapter—at the core of SPSCM. Demand for service parts is not driven by planned sales orders but by unpredictable service events—failures, preventive maintenance, part recalls, or customer upgrades—that vary by geography, season, product maturity, and installed base utilization.

For instance:

- A sudden spike in failures for a specific component—due to a supplier quality issue—can overwhelm local stockrooms if not detected early.
- Demand shifts as products move from warranty into extended service contracts, which may change the criticality and mix of needed parts.
- Preventive maintenance campaigns create planned but time-bound demand surges that must be absorbed at the local or regional level.

These fluctuations are amplified in a multi-echelon system because each tier relies on forecasting downstream consumption across a broader time horizon and spatial footprint. A misalignment in just one node, for example, can create ripple effects across the entire network—leading to excess inventory at one level and critical stockouts at another.

To counteract this, successful SPSCM operations deploy tiered safety stock models, dynamic lead time buffers, and real-time monitoring tools that continuously adjust stocking levels based on observed failure rates and SLA compliance metrics. Still, the inherent variability of demand remains a fundamental challenge that makes multi-echelon planning one of the most complex elements of global SPSCM.

Chapter Summary:
Integrating Inventory Strategy into SPSCM Resilience

The multi-echelon inventory network is a cornerstone of effective SPSCM operations. It enables OEMs to:

- Meet SLA commitments across a fragmented global customer base
- Optimize inventory placement and capital investment
- Adapt to region-specific regulations and infrastructure constraints

Unlike FSCM, where inventory is based on predictable sales patterns, SPSCM networks must flex with real-time service events, local restrictions, and evolving entitlement profiles. In the semiconductor industry and other high-tech sectors, this flexibility is essential to sustaining uptime and service profitability.

As products age, service contracts expire, and new technologies emerge, the network must evolve. Effective SPSCM leaders treat the multi-echelon structure not as a static model, but as a dynamic, data-driven system—one that continuously learns from service activity, entitlement data, and regional demand patterns to proactively stay ahead of disruptions.

Chapter 10

Challenge #4:
Inventory Control

Navigating the Complexities of Inventory Management in SPSCM

SPSCM operates under a fundamentally different set of rules than traditional forward supply chains. At the heart of the distinction is the challenge of inventory control in an environment defined by unpredictability, long-tail demand, and stringent service level expectations.

This chapter explores three core areas critical to effective SPSCM inventory control execution: **part chaining, repair and refurbishment**, and the delicate balance between **inflows and exit points** of service parts in the operation. While each of these areas presents distinct operational considerations, they are deeply interconnected and collectively shape the overall efficiency and resilience of the service network.

This chapter begins by unpacking inventory control functions, highlighting the consequences of overstocking and understocking within supply chains where obsolescence is high and disposal options are limited.

It then introduces **part chaining** as a strategic tool to extend inventory usability across generations of product—mitigating excess and enabling broader fulfillment flexibility.

The discussion on **repair and refurbishment** highlights the importance of managing reverse logistics and repair yields across three dimensions: physical, functional, and systemic success rates.

Finally, the concept of **inflows and exit points** is examined as a critical control level, underscoring the importance of proactive material introduction and the scarcity of viable exit options once inventory is in the network.

Together these themes illustrate the unique operational pressure SPSCM faces—and why managing them in harmony is key to long-term service and financial performance.

The Fundamentals of Inventory Control in SPSCM

In SPSCM, inventory control plays a central role in balancing service readiness with cost efficiency. The organization has to manage through extended lifecycles, combined with erratic and low-volume demand, making overstocking and understocking uniquely problematic.

Overstocking in SPSCM carries more severe consequences than traditional supply chain. When excess service parts accumulate, they rarely have alternative uses. Unlike FSCM where surplus finished goods can often be repackaged, resold, or redirected to alternative sales channels, most service parts are highly specialized and compatible with only a specific set of products and configurations. This limits the ability to liquidate excess stock. Worse still, many service parts are at risk of technological obsolescence—rendering them useless when their corresponding equipment becomes obsolete or is no longer supported.

Because exit points for unused inventory are limited, companies often resort to warehousing obsolete parts, absorbing ongoing carrying costs with no real prospects of consumption. This can have a compounding effect across regions and stocking locations, particularly in multi-echelon networks where inventory visibility and redistribution mechanisms may be weak or delayed.

Understocking, conversely, threatens service levels and contractual obligations. When inventory is unavailable at the time of need—especially for critical systems or high-priority customers—it can result in penalties, reputational damage, or lost business. Unlike traditional supply chains where production cycles can be ramped up to recover from stockouts, SPSCM often deals with parts that are no longer manufactured, require long lead times, or must be sourced through repair and refurbishment. The ability to react quickly is diminished, making proactive inventory planning not just beneficial, but essential.

To further complicate matters, many service parts are "slow-movers"—they experience long intervals between demand events, often with high variability. This makes traditional forecasting methods less reliable. Inventory planners must therefore rely on a combination of failure rate modeling, installed base analysis, service history, and lifecycle stage assessments to develop more accurate stocking strategies.

The implications are clear: SPSCM organizations must treat every inflow supply decision with greater scrutiny—a challenge given the unpredictability of demand. Overstocking ties up capital and risks obsolescence, while understocking exposes the business to service failure. Managing this delicate balance requires advanced planning systems, tight governance over inflows, and a highly coordinated view of field demand, product lifecycle curves, and inventory reusability. We will walk through three operational processes that many advanced SPSCM organizations utilize to maintain the balance.

Linking Parts Through Chaining in SPSCM

In SPSCM, maintaining operational continuity hinges on the availability and efficient management of tens of thousands of service parts. In many large OEMs, the number of unique part numbers can exceed 100,000, spanning multiple product lines, geographies, and generations of technology. This breadth introduces a critical challenge in inventory management: parts that are functionally equivalent or interchangeable must be linked and managed intelligently to avoid duplication, minimize cost, and ensure rapid service fulfillment.

The foundation of these interrelationships is built during the product design and manufacturing stages. Engineering teams often apply the principle of component reuse—leveraging proven parts from earlier product generations to ensure performance continuity, reduce R&D overhead, and improve manufacturing efficiency. As products evolve, parts may be updated or enhanced based on cost targets, supplier changes, or performance improvements. Others may be configurable, supporting customer-specific requirements. In SPSCM, these technical relationships are formalized through a process known as **part chaining**.

What is Part Chaining?

Part chaining is the practice of mapping predefined relationships between parts that are similar, compatible, or interchangeable. These relationships allow planners and service professionals to substitute parts intelligently, ensuring availability without violating performance standards or customer entitlements. Part chaining is especially vital when managing aging products, long service lifecycles, or constrained supplier environments.

Types of Part Chains

Part chains typically fall into two broad categories:

1. **One-Way Chain**

   - A newer part may substitute for an older part, but not the other way around.
   - *Example*: If a laptop originally shipped with a 50 GB Seagate hard drive, and only 100 GB versions are available, the 100 GB

drive may be used as a replacement. However, replacing a 100 GB drive with a 50 GB drive would result in reduced performance and is not acceptable.

- One-way chaining helps phase out obsolete parts while minimizing unnecessary inventory of legacy components.

2. **Two-Way Chain**

- Parts are fully interchangeable in both directions.
- *Example*: A 100 GB Seagate and a 100 GB SanDisk drive may be used interchangeably depending on supplier lead time, cost, or regional availability.
- This provides planners greater flexibility in sourcing and helps mitigate supply risks.

Characteristics and Complexity of Part Chains

Part chains in SPSCM can be highly intricate, often involving dozens or even hundreds of related parts across product lines, generations, or configurations. A single line might contain chains with mixed one-way and two-way relationships, creating a branching tree of substitutions. Managing this complexity requires:

- Clear documentation of compatibility rules
- Coordination with engineering, sourcing, and compliance teams
- Systems capable of dynamic substitution logic during service planning

Example: A Toshiba-branded drive may only be replaced with newer Toshiba models in a one-way relationship, while the same Toshiba drive may be used interchangeably in other systems with broader two-way compatibility allowances.

In regulated industries—such as aerospace, defense, or healthcare—part chains are further constrained. Government contracts may mandate domestic sourcing, creating separate part numbers for otherwise identical parts sourced from approved suppliers. These restrictions must be reflected in part chain logic to ensure compliance and avoid service disruptions.

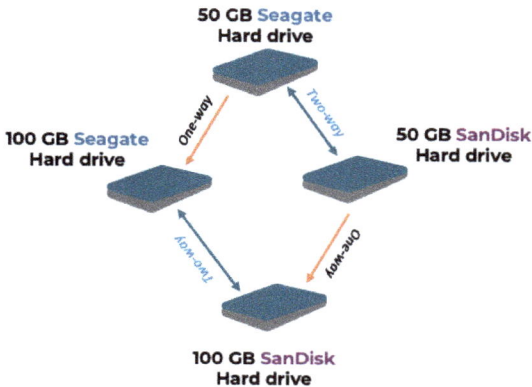

50 GB Seagate
Hard drive

100 GB Seagate
Hard drive

50 GB SanDisk
Hard drive

100 GB SanDisk
Hard drive

Note: The 100 GB SanDisk drive (bottom) has a one-way relationship with both the 50 GB SanDisk drive and the 50 GB Seagate drive (at top). It also has a two-way relationship with the 100GB Seagate drive.

Strategic Importance of Part Chaining in SPSCM

Effectively managing part chains offers multiple benefits across the product lifecycle:

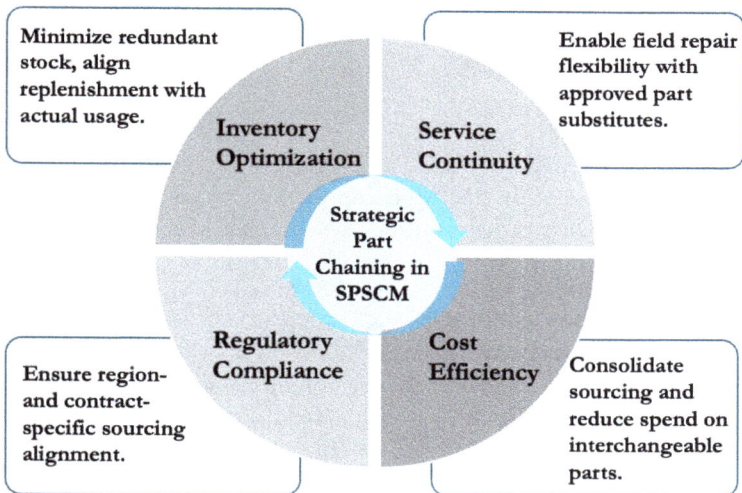

Minimize redundant stock, align replenishment with actual usage.

Inventory Optimization

Enable field repair flexibility with approved part substitutes.

Service Continuity

Strategic Part Chaining in SPSCM

Ensure region- and contract-specific sourcing alignment.

Regulatory Compliance

Cost Efficiency

Consolidate sourcing and reduce spend on interchangeable parts.

Neglecting part chaining often results in excess inventory, reactive procurement, and delayed service delivery—symptoms that are typically identified only during costly root-cause analyses.

Moreover, part chaining expertise is not easily replaced. Professionals skilled in chain mapping, service entitlement interpretation, and cross-functional coordination play a vital role in sustaining SPSCM resilience. Retaining this knowledge can be a source of long-term competitive advantage.

In Summary

Part chaining is a hallmark of advanced SPSCM operations. It transforms fragmented inventories into cohesive, flexible systems capable of adapting to product evolution, supply variability, and regional constraints. By formalizing the logic of interchangeability, organizations unlock significant benefits: streamlined inventory, reduced cost, and improved service performance.

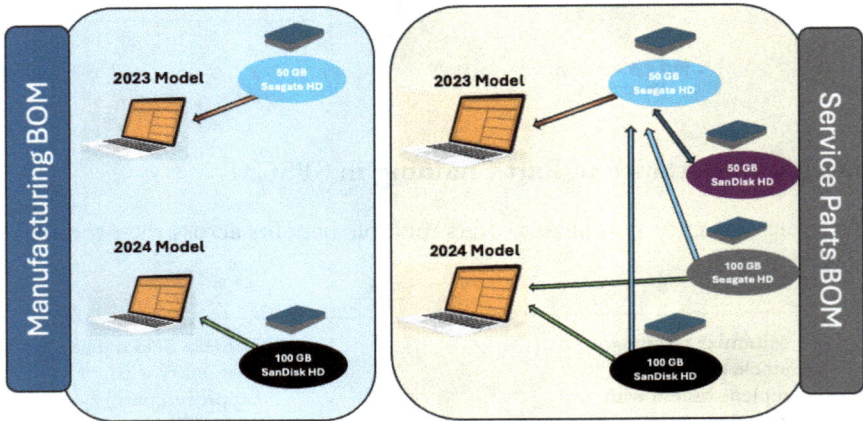

Manufacturing BOM versus Service Parts BOM

Respectively, part chaining in SPSCM is far more complex than in forward supply chain management. In FSCM, components typically flow through a controlled manufacturing process with clearly defined bills of materials and minimal substitution.

In contrast, SPSCM must support part substitutions across multiple generations of products, variable configurations, regional compliance requirements, and unpredictable service events—all while ensuring performance and contractual alignment. Chains must accommodate forward and backward compatibility, version control, and real-world service realities that FSCM systems rarely face.

As service networks grow and products become more complex, the need for structured dynamic part chaining will only increase. Forward-looking SPSCM leaders treat it not as a technical detail but as a strategic discipline—essential to sustaining global service excellence.

Repair and Refurbishment in Service Parts Supply Chain Management

A fundamental challenge in SPSCM is optimizing inventory levels while meeting service performance targets. One of the most effective strategies for achieving this balance is by leveraging repaired and refurbished parts as substitutes for new ones. In contrast to FSCM, where returned products are incidental in nature, the repair and refurbishment of service parts is a core strategy in SPSCM, deeply embedded in day-to-day operations. These activities fall within the domains of **reverse logistics**, or **reverse supply chain**.

In this segment, we explore the strategic role of repairs and refurbishment, how they differ from FSCM practices, and the operational complexities involved in executing them effectively.

Reverse Supply Chain in FSCM versus SPSCM

In FSCM, reverse logistics generally refers to handling customer returns due to dissatisfaction, defects, shipping errors, or end-of-life product disposal. Returns are tracked through **Return Material Authorizations (RMAs)** and are often resold, refurbished for secondary markets, or scrapped depending on quality and cost-effectiveness. However, FSCM rarely depends on returns to fulfill forward demand.

In contrast, **SPSCM depends heavily on reverse logistics**—not just as a corrective mechanism, but as a proactive and essential source of service parts. Repair and refurbishment enable service teams to meet warranty obligations, reduce material costs, and support circular economy initiatives. This approach is especially critical in mature lifecycle stages, where new parts may be unavailable, expensive, or slower to procure.

Unique Dynamics of Repair & Refurbishment in SPSCM

Unlike FSCM, where returned products may be scrapped or sold as-is, **SPSCM organizations systematically capture, repair, and redeploy service parts**. Policies are developed to identify which parts to return. Examples include:

- Low-cost, consumable items (e.g., cables, gaskets) are typically scrapped on-site.
- High-value, complex components (e.g., circuit boards, compressors, motors) are routed to repair centers for evaluation and refurbishment.

For example, when an OEM services a business-grade laptop under warranty, a refurbished motherboard may be installed instead of a new one—delivering the same functionality at a significantly lower cost, and typically without the customer noticing any difference.

This process delivers several benefits:

- Up to **30%-70% cost savings** compared to new parts
- Reduced dependency on upstream suppliers and lead times
- Lower environmental impact through component reuse

Use Case: Computing Industry

In the computing industry, particularly among enterprise OEMs (e.g., servers, storage, and networking), repair and refurbishment play a mission-critical role.

Consider an enterprise service OEM that supports a five-year hardware warranty for its mid-range storage systems. A failed RAID controller card is returned by the field technician. The defective part is:

1. Tagged and returned via RMA to the OEM's return warehouse
2. Inspected to determine if it's repairable
3. Sent to a third-party vendor specializing in microelectronics
4. After successful repair and testing, re-enters inventory as a **certified refurbished**
5. Deployed again in a future service call—possibly within days or weeks

This cycle ensures lower cost per service event, maintains SLA compliance, and enables the OEM to manage inventory more predictably. Meanwhile, global operations must account for **regulatory constraints, repair vendor performance**, and **regional return rates**, adding complexity to forecasting and planning.

Service Parts Supply Chain Reverse Logistics

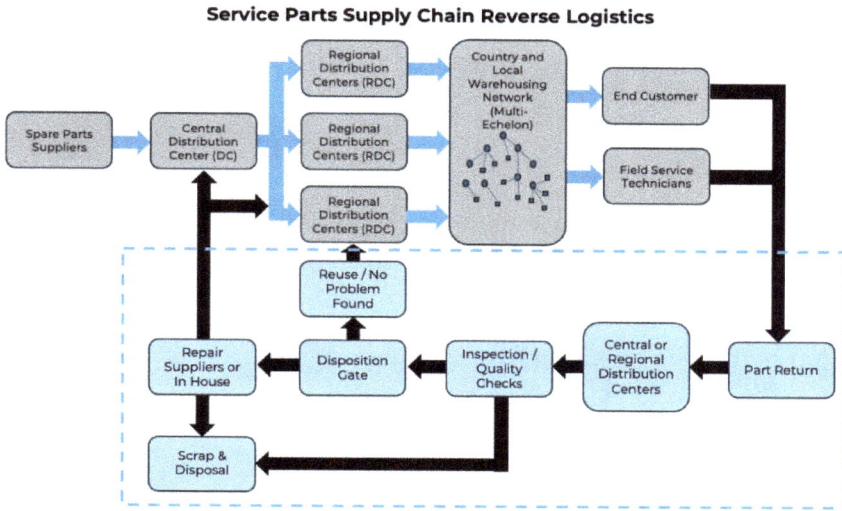

Key Operational Challenges in the SPSCM Repair Process

While the use of repaired and refurbished parts offers significant advantages in cost savings and sustainability, executing this strategy effectively involves navigating several complex operational hurdles. Unlike traditional inventory replenishment models, repair-driven supply chains must account for uncertainty and variability across multiple stages—beginning with part returns from the field, followed by inspection for repair viability, and ending with actual repair execution by suppliers. Each stage introduces potential yield losses that can disrupt inventory forecasts and service readiness.

Understanding and managing these challenges is critical for optimizing repair inventory flows and achieving a sustainable repair-to-new buy ratio over the product lifecycle. The multiple stages are:

1. Field Return Rate Yield

Repair strategies rely on getting failed parts back from the field. Return rates vary dramatically by geography and operational discipline:

Global Field Returns Yield Map

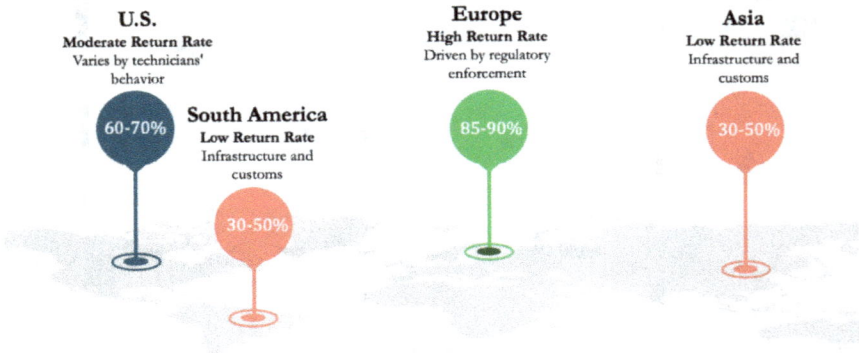

U.S.
Moderate Return Rate
Varies by technicians'
behavior

60-70%

South America
Low Return Rate
Infrastructure and
customs

30-50%

Europe
High Return Rate
Driven by regulatory
enforcement

85-90%

Asia
Low Return Rate
Infrastructure and
customs

30-50%

Why Field Returns Matter	
Small Repair Pool	Fewer parts eligible for repair
Increased New Buys	Overbuying due to return shortfall.
Forecast Disruption	Planning impact from unpredictable returns

Delays or failures in returning parts reduce the pool of repairable items, forcing organizations to overbuy new parts unnecessarily.

2. Inspection Yield

Not all returned parts are salvageable. Some are too damaged or obsolete to repair. Inspection yield—the percentage of parts that pass quality checks—must be built into inventory planning models to forecast usable stock accurately.

3. Repair Supplier Yield Rate

Even parts that pass inspection may fail at the repair center due to component damage, unavailability of sub-parts, or cost-inefficiency. Accurate planning must consider:

- Historical repair success rates per part type
- Vendor-specific performance metrics
- Repair time variability and return lead times

Even after passing inspection, some parts may still be deemed unrepairable due to damage or cost constraints. Planners must account for supplier repair yield rates to maintain an accurate inventory replenishment strategy.

By considering all three yield stages—field returns, inspections, and repair supplier rates—planners can accurately estimate repairable stock availability, reducing unnecessary new purchases.

Repairable parts supply chain

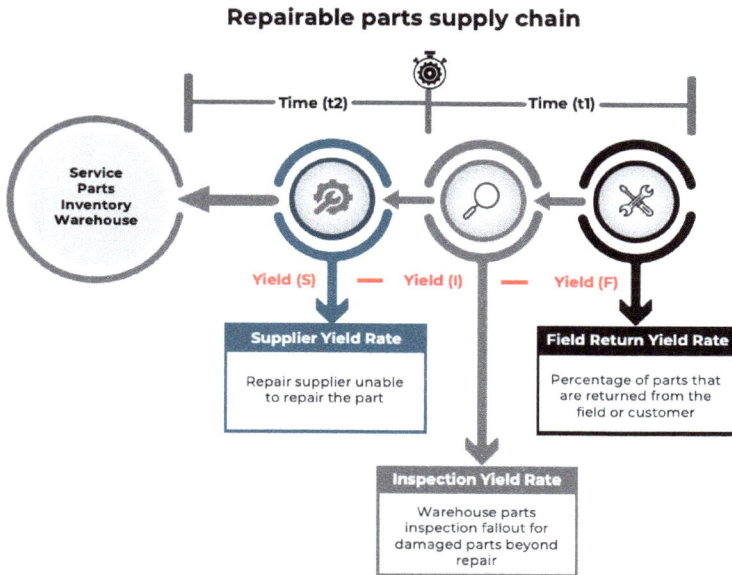

These three yield rates—field return yield, inspection yield, and repair supplier yield—are multiplicative in nature, meaning that the effective availability of repairable parts is the product of all three. This compounding effect can drastically reduce the final pool of usable inventory. For instance, a strong repair supplier yield is irrelevant if field return compliance is poor. Moreover, delays in any step—especially in the initial part return from the field—can create ripple effects that derail inventory forecasts and force urgent new part purchases, increasing cost and lead times.

This is not a passive process; it must be proactively managed across teams and geographies, often requiring real-time coordination, feedback loops, and exception handling. Planning for repaired parts, therefore, is not just a matter of inventory flow—it's a high-precision balancing act that depends on cross-functional execution and disciplined operational oversight.

Managing the Repair-to-New Buy Ratio

As a product matures, the sourcing mix gradually shifts from mostly new parts to a balance heavily weighted toward refurbished ones:

New Part versus Repaired Part Purchase Ratio

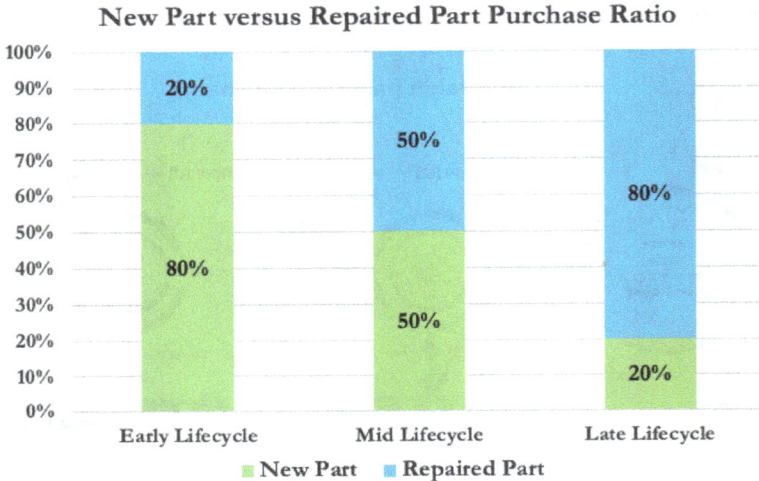

- **Early lifecycle**: New part dominant (limited returns and urgent demand)
- **Mid lifecycle**: Evenly split as returns are more concentrated and buffer stocks stabilize
- **Late lifecycle**: Repair parts become the dominant source, to minimize inflow of new material

Transitioning to this optimized state requires:

- Yield modeling across all three stages (field, inspection, repair)
- Reliable reverse logistics
- Repair SLA enforcement
- Clear incentives for field technicians to return parts promptly (e.g., credit awards, penalties for non-compliance)

Regional and Global Regulatory Complexities

Global SPSCM networks must navigate diverse **regulatory landscapes** that impact repair operations:

- **Brazil and India:** Strict laws prohibit the import of used or repaired parts, necessitating localized repair centers.

- **Europe:** Must comply with **WEEE (Waste Electrical and Electronic Equipment)** directives
- **North America:** Often driven by cost-efficiency and technician compliance rather than regulation

These regional dynamics increase the need for decentralized planning and regional inventory strategies.

In Summary

Incorporating repaired and refurbished parts into SPSCM offers significant cost savings, sustainability benefits, and operational flexibility. However, achieving these benefits requires more than just identifying repairable units—it demands a disciplined, data-driven approach across multiple operational touchpoints. The repair lifecycle hinges on three additive yield stages:

- Field return rates
- Inspection success rate
- Repair supplier yields.

These stages are interdependent and compounding—meaning a breakdown or delay in one of them can derail repair planning, leading to shortages and force unplanned new purchases.

Managing Inflows and Exit Points: A Core Challenge in SPSCM

One of the most persistent and underestimated challenges in SPSCM is managing inventory inflows and exit points. In contrast to traditional FSCM, where product demand forecasting drives supply, SPSCM must plan for uncertain, sporadic, and long-tail demand that may not materialize for years—if at all. This unpredictability, combined with tight service level agreements (SLAs), forces SPSCM planning to proactively introduce parts into the network with little assurance of future consumption. **Once inventory enters the service network, safely exiting that stock becomes exponentially more difficult.**

At its core, the objective is simple but elusive: introduce inventory into the network at the right time and in the right quantity—without overstocking or starving demand. But unlike FSCM, which has a clearer linkage between production and sales, SPSCM operates in a highly reactive environment. This imbalance between inflows and exit opportunities is one of the defining operational hurdles in SPSCM.

For a moment, think of the supply chain as a black box, with demand (orders) as its output. In a simplified model, the supply chain's role is to match that output with the inflow of material required to fulfill demand. The goal is to balance these points as closely as possible, bringing in just enough material to achieve alignment.

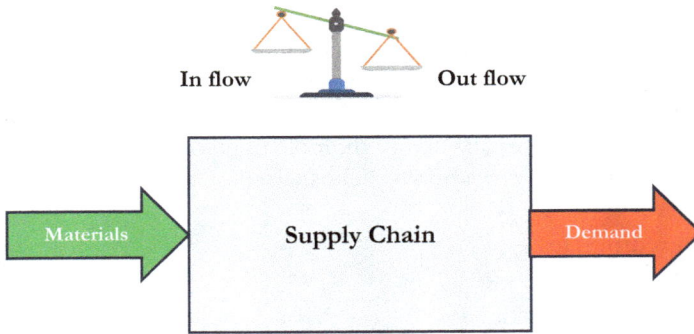

A key point to highlight is that the supply chain has little control over when demand will occur. The only real lever available to maintain balance is controlling the inflow of materials.

Let's now expand this simplified example and compare how FSCM and the SPSCM manage this balance.

Forward Supply Chain Inflows and Exit Points

In the forward supply chain, inflows of raw materials and components are tied to production schedules based on forecasted customer orders. The movement of raw materials and components through manufacturing is largely controlled and linear. If forecasts are wrong and demand drops, several corrective levers are available: pause or cancel orders, slow down production, or liquidate finished goods through resale channels or discounts.

Inventory in FSCM typically resides in one of three stages:

1. **In-Flow Supply**: Purchase orders and staging materials
2. **Work-in-Process (WIP)**: Semi-completed goods on the production line
3. **Finished Goods**: Ready-to-sell inventory held in distribution centers

Inflow and Exit of the Forward Supply Chain

If excess builds up, FSCM organizations can:

- **Divert new components and raw materials**:
  - o Store and reuse in future production
  - o Continue feeding manufacturing to use up materials
  - o Sell on the open market
- **Continue to feed manufacturing WIP:**
  - o Complete production and transfer to finished goods
- **Convert WIP to finished goods:**
  - o Sell at a discount to customers
  - o Sell to resellers at reduced prices

With multiple exit options, the forward supply chain has several mechanisms for regaining control over misaligned inflow and demand, helping to avoid deep financial write-offs.

Service Parts Supply Chain:
Unpredictable Demand, Few Exits

In contrast, SPSCM must proactively stock parts based on predictive models and installed base estimates, often years in advance of demand. This primary—and often only—exit point is a service event: either a customer or field technician requires the part. However, SPSCM planners have little control over the timing or volume of these service events.

Inventory management is further complicated by repair and refurbishment reverse logistics, which must be balanced to reduce new part purchases and optimize overall stock levels. Think of the SPSCM inventory control system as a closed loop for parts that have repairability. If a new part enters inventory that is eligible to be repaired once consumed, then that broken part is essentially part of the closed loop system as a less expensive alternative supplier source to offset a new part entering the loop. Oftentimes, that repairable item can be refurbished multiple times, which supports effective cost control practices and environmental stewardship.

In addition, service parts are typically only valuable to those servicing or owning the specific supported product. While some parts may be shared across similar products, they usually represent a small portion of total inventory cost.

Inflow and Exit of a Service Supply Chain

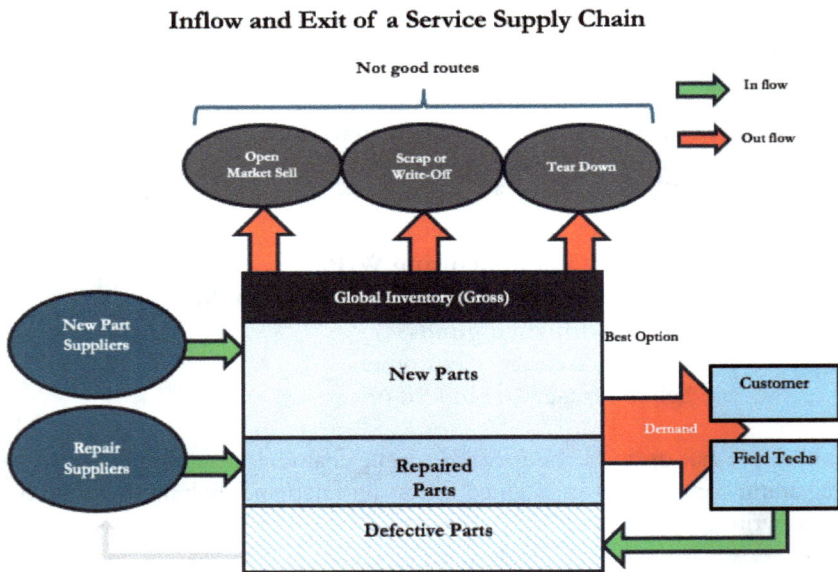

Furthermore, once inventory enters SPSCM, exit options are extremely limited:

- **Sell to clients at a discount**—though this may cannibalize future product sales.
- **Offer free upgrades**—raising financial exposure and support costs.
- **Tear down for salvageable components**—often labor-intensive and low yield.

- **Sell on the open market**—usually at steep discounts and only for select parts.
- **Scrap and write-off**—the most common, yet most wasteful, outcome.

This limited exit flexibility makes controlling the inflow of materials the single most important lever available to SPSCM teams. Overestimating demand or misjudging the timing of part needs often results in stockpiles of unused inventory that remain on the books indefinitely.

This fundamental difference explains why SPSC will never achieve the same inventory efficiency as the forward supply chain. Once inventory enters the SPSC, few viable exit options remain unless demand increases—a factor SPSCM cannot directly influence.

Use Case: Telecom Equipment Support

Consider a global telecom company that supports network hardware across a ten-year lifecycle. For legacy routers, planning must stock parts long after the equipment has been discontinued. Initially, demand is predictable as units fail under warranty. But once the product ages, usage rates become erratic, and forecasting grows more uncertain. Despite this, SLAs require the company to maintain high part availability across multiple regions.

After five years, the company identifies that over $5M of service inventory is sitting idle with no signs of future demand. Attempts to exit the inventory through resale and teardown are unsuccessful. In the end, the company is forced to write off 70% of the value—resulting from an initial inflow miscalculation made years earlier.

Long Product Lifecycles: Hidden Risks of Accumulation

Longer product lifecycles further complicate inflow-exit dynamics. While extended support timelines provide value to customers, they also prolong the inventory liability period—the time during which unused inventory must be carried on the books. Stock introduced early in the lifecycle may sit unused for years, leading to excess accumulation. Often, companies choose to hold inventory in hopes of future consumption rather than writing it off—especially when disposal options are limited.

The problem intensifies when excess is fragmented across a global network. Without centralized visibility and harmonized planning processes, regional teams may continue ordering parts already overstocked elsewhere in the network.

Strategies to Tighten Inflow Control

To avoid downstream accumulation, leading SPSCM organizations focus on proactively managing material inflows. Key strategies include:

- **Maximizing repair and refurbishment**, reducing the need for new buy inflows
- **Rebalancing excess inventory** across global and regional nodes
- **Using installed base analytics and advanced demand models** to refine forecasts
- **Applying part chaining logic** to extend usability of legacy inventory across generations.
- **Implementing strict inflow gates** where planners must justify material buys against existing stock

These practices shift SPSCM operations from reactive inventory correction to proactive inflow prevention—an essential pivot in achieving long-term efficiency.

Closing: Why Inflow-Exit Discipline Is a Strategic Imperative

Effectively managing inventory inflows and exit points in SPSCM is not just an operational concern—it's a strategic imperative. The limited exit options in the service parts environment amplify the risks of overstocking and write-offs, especially when combined with long-tail demand and high SLA requirements.

Organizations that excel in this area do so by treating inflow control as a disciplined, cross-functional process—integrating forecasting, repair, and parts reuse strategies to reduce waste and ensure service readiness.

In a world with limited internal levers of control available, inflow management remains one of the few areas where SPSCM teams can drive measurable impact. When managed well, it becomes a powerful enabler of cost control, inventory efficiency, and world-class service performance.

Closing Chapter Summary: Inventory Levers for Proactive Service Inventory Management

As this chapter demonstrates, effective inventory management in SPSCM requires more than just accurate forecasting—it demands a system of interconnected levers working in concert. Part chaining extends the value of legacy inventory, allowing service organizations to satisfy demand across product families with fewer SKUs. Repair and refurbishment programs reduce reliance on new inflows, but they must be carefully managed to account for variable yields and quality outcomes. Meanwhile, inflow control remains the most direct and impactful mechanism to prevent the buildup of slow-moving or obsolete parts.

The key challenge lies in the fact that once service inventory enters the network, very few exit points exist. This forces organizations to adopt a preventative mindset rather than a corrective one. It's no longer sufficient to "optimize later"—every inflow decision must be scrutinized at the outset with lifecycle planning, installed base alignment, and consumption modeling.

Ultimately, SPSCM success hinges on mastering these internal levers. In a supply chain where demand is volatile and exit options are constrained, excellence depends on how well an organization anticipates, reuses, and reallocates inventory—before problems arise. The practices discussed in this chapter offer a glimpse of the type of challenges SPSCM faces to demonstrate a level of control and resilience, empowering service organizations to meet SLAs, reduce waste, and manage costs—without compromising on availability.

Chapter 11

Challenge #5:
The Impact of Product Entitlements on SPSCM

Among the most overlooked but critical challenges in SPSCM is the dynamic nature of **product entitlements**—warranties, service contracts, or out-of-coverage statuses tied to equipment in the field. As equipment moves through its lifecycle, its entitlement profile evolves, creating a constantly shifting landscape of support obligations that must be matched by inventory and logistic strategies. In industries where uptime is paramount, such as semiconductor manufacturing or heavy machinery, these entitlement variations can introduce significant planning complexity and financial risk.

Entitlements and the Installed Base:
A Dual Forecasting Challenge

Installed base location is a foundational element of accurate service parts forecasting, but it only tells part of the story. Equally important is understanding **what type of service coverage** applies to each installed system. A machine under a full-service contract with a 95% uptime SLA demands radically different support than one with no entitlement or a basic warranty.

As systems age and transition between support tiers—or move between customers—entitlement shifts create a mosaic of requirements that inventory planners must track and predict. A failure to capture these changes can result in excess inventory in low-risk regions or, worse, stockouts in locations where high-entitlement-driven demand occurs.

Semiconductor OEM Use Case:
Uptime Pressure and Entitlement Complexity

Semiconductor manufacturing offers a vivid example of these challenges. Equipment OEMs often serve customers with aggressive uptime guarantees—commonly 95% or more—which translates to just **36 hours of allowable unscheduled downtime per month** on average. In this environment, even a

48-hour delay for a critical part can exhaust the monthly downtime allowance and trigger SLA penalties.

Compounding the issue is the nature of semiconductor tools: hundreds of potential failure points, highly specialized parts, and a wide range of system ages and entitlements spread across the globe. A planner may be responsible for simultaneously supporting a brand-new tool under a platinum contract in Singapore and a fifteen-year-old system in a remote Italian fab with minimal support. Each situation demands a different service model, stocking strategy, and cost-risk trade-off.

To expand on this scenario, a semiconductor OEM faced a dilemma in Italy, where the majority of the installed base was centered in Rome, but key satellite systems were located in Milan—**a 7.5-hour drive from the central stockroom**. While Florence was more geographically central, Rome's largest demand concentration dictated stocking decisions, leaving Milan exposed. With a high-SLA customer operating in Milan, the OEM has to establish a secondary stocking location, incurring additional cost and operational complexity—justified solely by the entitlement risk tied to that customer.

Inventory Network for Italy

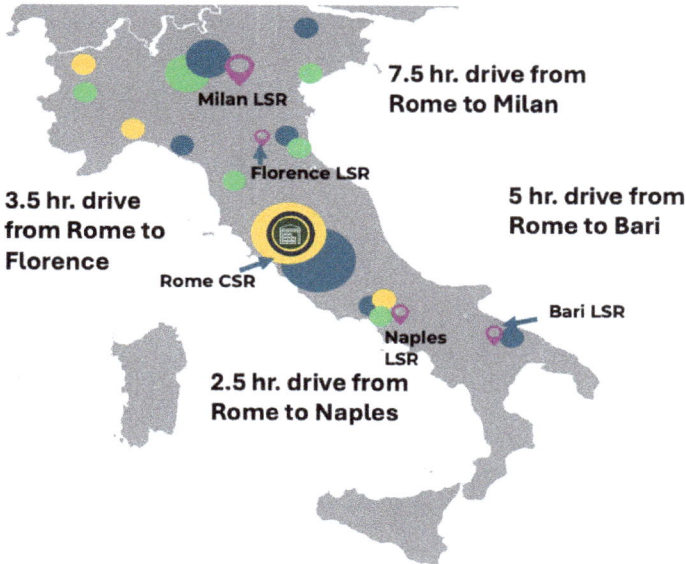

Milan LSR

7.5 hr. drive from Rome to Milan

Florence LSR

3.5 hr. drive from Rome to Florence

5 hr. drive from Rome to Bari

Rome CSR

Bari LSR

Naples LSR

2.5 hr. drive from Rome to Naples

Inventory Strategy: Balancing Uptime, Geography, and Cost

Providing 97-99% part availability to meet high SLAs is not only operationally difficult—it's economically painful. Semiconductor OEMs often deal with long part lead times (three to nine months), expensive components, and globally distributed customers. Increasing part availability by even **1% can translate into tens of millions of dollars** annually in additional inventory and holding costs.

To manage this, OEMs adopt multi-echelon inventory strategies, segmenting parts by:

- **Failure criticality**
- **Usage frequency**
- **Entitlement tier**
- **Geographical proximity**

This segmentation enables differentiated stocking approaches, from centrally held stock for non-critical parts to customer-site consignment inventory for high-risk high-SLA contracts.

The Role of Field Technicians and Real-Time Responsiveness

Technicians are the front-line enablers of SLA compliance. Their ability to diagnose failures quickly and initiate part orders with minimal delay directly affects whether a service event falls within the SLA window. Delays in triage or misdiagnosed issues often lead to cascading service delays and missed commitments.

In some high-risk locations, OEMs turn to on-site consignment inventory to bypass these challenges. While costly, this ensures immediate part availability and removes dependency on transportation or warehouse lead times.

Lifecycle Transitions and Strategic Reassessment

As products age, entitlements change. Some customers let contracts expire, others renew or upgrade to premium tiers. With each shift, **inventory strategies must be revalidated**. Earlier decisions—such as offering 95% uptime guarantees to penetrate a new region—can lock the OEM into long-term support burdens that require sustained stocking, logistics, and technician coverage for years.

Moreover, failure rates fluctuate across the product lifecycle. Some components may become less reliable with age, while others experience infant mortality early in deployment. These shifting patterns demand dynamic, data-driven forecasting models and close alignment between customer engagement, field service, and supply chain planning.

In Summary: Navigating Entitlement-Driven Complexity

The integration of product entitlements into SPSCM's dynamic demand equation elevates the complexity into a multi-dimensional optimization challenge. Semiconductor OEMs, as an example, must navigate:

- High-uptime contractual obligations
- Globally dispersed installed bases
- Entitlement tiers that constantly evolve
- Financial pressures tied to inventory availability

To succeed, organizations must combine **deep entitlement visibility** with dynamic, responsive inventory strategies that evolve alongside the product lifecycle and customer needs. Only by acknowledging and planning for the full implications of entitlement complexity can OEMs balance performance, customer satisfaction, and cost efficiency across the global service network.

Section Conclusion:
Navigating the Five Core Challenges of SPSCM

SPSCM is one of the most complex operational domains due to the inherent unpredictability of demand, long product lifecycles, and the high stakes of service-level performance. This section has examined five foundational challenges that define the SPSCM landscape and explored how each one uniquely shapes planning, execution, and strategic decision-making.

1. **Diversity of Service Models**
   The first challenge stems from the wide range of service delivery models—ranging from advanced replacement to field repair to depot service. Each model carries different part availability expectations, inventory positioning requirements, and logistics constraints. OEMs must design supply chains that are flexible enough to accommodate this diversity while still maintaining cost and service performance across global operations.

2. **Dynamics of SPSCM Demand Forecasting**
   Unlike FSCM, where forecasts are tied to production or sales, SPSCM demand is driven by uncertain failure patterns, customer usage behavior,

and variable service entitlements. Forecasting in this environment requires sophisticated models that account for intermittent demand, multi-echelon dependencies, and real-time field data. Without accurate forecasting, service levels deteriorate, and inventory costs escalate.

3. **OEM Field Repair and Maintenance Multi-Echelon Networks**
   In high-complexity industries like semiconductor equipment manufacturing, the field repair network often spans multiple geographies and stocking levels. Planners must balance new part purchases with returns, repairs, and refurbishments—each with its own yield rate and lead time. The result is a complex closed-loop system where even small disruptions—such as delayed returns or repair failures—can ripple through the network and disrupt planning accuracy.

4. **Inventory Control and Exit Strategy Limitations**
   Service parts inventory, once introduced into the network, is difficult to exit. Unlike FSCM, which can repurpose, discount, or liquidate inventory, service parts often become obsolete or product specific. Misalignment between inflows and actual demand leads to costly overstocking, especially when global regions operate without tight process synchronization. Managing inflows, rebalancing excess inventory, and leveraging tactics like part chaining and repair are critical levers for controlling cost and improving responsiveness.

5. **Impact of Product Entitlements on SPSCM**
   The final challenge centers on the evolving nature of product entitlements—warranties, service contracts, or out-of-coverage statuses—and how they influence service expectations. High-uptime SLAs drive the need for localized stocking and faster response times, while legacy systems under minimal support create different requirements. OEMs must dynamically adjust stocking strategies and field technician enablement to meet these contractual commitments without incurring excessive cost.

Final Thoughts

Mastering SPSCM requires more than technical execution, it demands a deep understanding of service strategy, lifecycle dynamics, and customer expectations. The five challenges explored in this section are not isolated—they are deeply interconnected. Poor demand forecasting increases inventory pressure. Mismanaged entitlements lead to SLA violations. A lack of field integration distorts network visibility.

To build resilient and cost-effective supply chains, organizations must approach SPSCM as a strategic capability—one that aligns cross-functional planning, leverages digital tools and analytics, and is tightly attuned to the shifting realities of installed base management. By tackling these five challenges head-on, OEMs can turn the service supply chain from a cost center into a competitive differentiator.

As we move into the next section of the book, we shift focus from internal structural challenges to the external forces and infrastructure that influence SPSCM performance. We'll explore how data-intensive execution forms the backbone of successful operations, how technology compatibility issues can either streamline or complicate service networks, and why SPSCM must be a company-wide priority to truly deliver on its promise. Understanding these broader systemic forces is essential for unlocking the full strategic value of the service part supply chain.

Part 3: Overview

How Infrastructure and External Forces Shape Service Parts Supply Chains

Up to this point, the focus has been on comparing the differences between Forward Supply Chain Management (FSCM) and Service Part Supply Chain Management (SPSCM) and examining the respective management processes involved. Additionally, we explored some of the challenges faced by SPSCM organizations—particularly in navigating interdependent and often misaligned variables necessary for efficient operations.

In this section, we will examine key infrastructure and external forces challenging the SPSCM's ability to deliver consistent performance in a robust and efficient manner. These challenges include:

- **Data as the Lifeblood of SPSCM: Visibility, Accuracy, and Operational Efficiency**
- **Technology as the Backbone of SPSCM: Aligning Systems for Performance**
- **Shared Ownership: How Cross-Functional Alignment Drives SPSCM Success**
- **Mergers, Acquisitions, and the Fragmentation Risk in SPSCM**

Chapter 12

Data as the Lifeblood of SPSCM:
Visibility, Accuracy, and Operational Efficiency

In SPSCM, data is more than just a supporting asset—it is the operational lifeblood. Every stocking decision, repair forecast, and SLA commitment depends on the quality, consistency, and timeliness of data flowing across multiple systems. While technology and infrastructure are important enablers, even the most advanced platforms fail to deliver results if the data feeding them is inaccurate or incomplete. In this chapter, we explore the central role of data in driving SPSCM effectiveness, the operational risks that stem from poor data quality, and why a strategic approach to data governance is essential to achieving true supply chain optimization.

Data: The Operational Backbone of SPSCM

Why SPSCM is Inherently Data-Intensive

SPSCM requires more data—and more types of data—than any other supply chain model. This is because it must account for a wide range of dynamic variables: unpredictable part failures, complex entitlement contracts, highly segmented service models, and geographically distributed inventories. Unlike traditional supply chains, which benefit from clearer demand signals and predictable replenishment cycles, SPSCM must make high-stakes decisions in an environment of uncertainty. This amplifies the reliance on data as a decision-making foundation.

Timely and Accurate Data Availability:
The Heartbeat of SPSCM

Regardless of whether a company uses advanced AI-powered platforms or manual spreadsheets, the outcome is only as good as the data feeding the system. In SPSCM, data drives three primary operational imperatives:

1. **Demand Forecasting:** Anticipating service parts requirements based on failure trends, installed base behavior, and maintenance schedules

2. **Inventory Management:** Setting safety stock levels, determining replenishment triggers, and optimizing distribution across a multi-echelon network

3. **Procurement and Planning:** Managing the inbound flow of new and refurbished service parts aligned to lead times and SLAs

If any of these decisions are made using outdated, incomplete, or misaligned data, the consequences ripple across the supply chain—leading to stockouts, excess inventory, SLA violations, and cost overruns.

Applying the Four V's of Big Data to SPSCM

To illustrate the nature of data requirements in SPSCM, it's helpful to examine them through the lens of the **Four V's**—with some tailored context:

1. **Veracity (Accuracy and Trustworthiness)**
   Data must accurately represent real-world conditions (e.g., correct part location, product status) and be auditable. Misrepresentation of data—such as overstated inventory or outdated entitlement records—creates false confidence and flawed planning.

2. **Velocity (Timeliness and Update Frequency)**
   In SPSCM, latency is the enemy. Data must reflect near-real-time events, particularly for parts movement, failure reports, and field service updates. Slow data creates blind spots that impair rapid response and resolution.

3. **Variety (Types and Sources of Data)**
   Data must be integrated across multiple systems (ERP, CRM, WMS, field service tools), each with its own format and structure. The more aligned and standardized this data is, the easier it becomes to generate cohesive insights and enable automation.

4. **Volume (Scale and Historical Reference)**
   With thousands of service parts and global demand events, SPSCM data sets are massive. These datasets must be both complete and organized—cataloged for trend analysis, root-cause identification, and long-term planning.

System Interdependencies: The SPSCM Data Ecosystem

The integrity of SPSCM data depends on the connectivity and synchronization across several enterprise systems:

- **Warehouse Management System (WMS):** Tracks parts movement, warehouse stock, and return logistics
- **Enterprise Resource Planning (ERP):** Handles procurement, vendor management, and financial records
- **Customer Relationship Management (CRM):** Captures customer contracts, installed base, and service entitlements
- **Field Service Platforms:** Logs service calls, parts usage, and technician performance
- **Product Engineering Databases:** Provides critical data for failure rate analysis and SPBOM configurations
- **Historical Data Warehouses:** Enables long-term trend analysis and lifecycle forecasting

Each system plays a role, and data misalignment between them can create planning conflicts, operational lags, and reporting errors.

The Impact of Data Gaps and Inaccuracies

Even small data inconsistencies can cascade into significant SPSCM inefficiencies.

Example: Installed Base Data Mismatch

Forecasting demand based on installed base planning assumes access to accurate records of where products are deployed and their entitlements. However, in many organizations, CRM systems are poorly maintained or only partially updated. This leads to:

- Overestimation or underestimation of demand
- Missed SLA stocking requirements
- Excess inventory in low-need regions and shortages in high-need ones

Without a clear understanding of where the installed base is located and its level of entitlement, SPSCM forecasting is at a clear disadvantage. The forecasting team must resort to using historical demand patterns which is not ideal, as it's equivalent of looking in the rearview mirror versus predicting what is ahead on the horizon.

Example: Supplier Lead Time Discrepancies

Safety stock calculations rely on lead time accuracy. If ERP data is outdated or incorrect, planners may set safety stock levels too low—leading to fulfillment failures—or too high—causing financial waste.

Global Data Alignment Challenges

For multinational organizations, regional systems often use different naming conventions, part numbering schemes, and data formats. This creates challenges in:

- Reconciling data across systems
- Harmonizing reporting for executive visibility
- Building scalable analytics or automation tools

Data Sharing and Technological Evolution

The transition from legacy, on-premise systems to cloud-based infrastructure has improved accessibility, but SPSCM still operates in hybrid environments. The ability to effectively share and update data across systems often defines whether an SPSCM organization is reactive or proactive.

Data Sharing Evolution

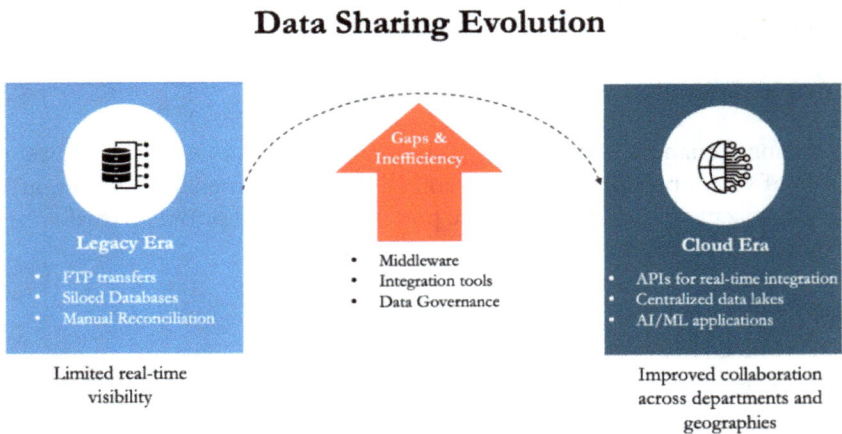

Legacy Era
- FTP transfers
- Siloed Databases
- Manual Reconciliation

Limited real-time visibility

Gaps & Inefficiency
- Middleware
- Integration tools
- Data Governance

Cloud Era
- APIs for real-time integration
- Centralized data lakes
- AI/ML applications

Improved collaboration across departments and geographies

However, many organizations still straddle both worlds, requiring investment in middleware, integration tools, and data governance strategies to bridge the gaps.

Use Case:
Resolving Data Misalignment in a Global SPSCM Network

Context

A global OEM in the medical equipment sector operated a complex SPSCM network supporting a large installed base across dozens of countries. This network included internal field teams, third-party providers, and regional distribution hubs. The company relied on a portfolio of enterprise systems, including ERP, CRM, WMS, field service platforms, and engineering databases.

Despite having advanced technology and a global footprint, the company was experiencing growing inefficiencies in meeting service level agreements and maintaining inventory availability across regions. Certain markets—especially those with regulatory and infrastructure complexities—were experiencing frequent part shortages, delayed repairs, and poor customer satisfaction outcomes.

Challenge

The root cause of these issues was found to be **fragmented, outdated, and misaligned data** across systems. Key pain points included:

- **Entitlement mismatches** in the CRM led to inaccurate stocking strategies in critical regions.
- **Installed base records** lacked sufficient detail on product configurations, making it difficult to forecast demand at the part variant level.
- **Supplier lead times** in the ERP were based on outdated assumptions, impacting safety stock calculations.
- **Reverse logistics** data was siloed, resulting in limited visibility into returned parts availability for repair and reuse.

These data issues created a ripple effect across the SPSCM—from inaccurate forecasting and understocking to increased reliance on expediting shipments and unplanned purchases of new parts.

Approach

To address the growing impact of data issues on supply chain performance, the company initiated a multi-phase remediation strategy involving cross-functional collaboration. Key steps included:

1. **Installed Base Revalidation**
    o Standardized and cleansed installed base records to include accurate location, entitlement, and configuration data
    o Automated synchronization across CRM and field service platforms
2. **Lead Time Realignment**
    o Updated supplier lead times using historical performance and external risk indicators
    o Refined replenishment policies to reflect true supply volatility
3. **Reverse Logistics Visibility**
    o Implemented a centralized control tower to monitor part returns in real-time
    o Improved technician compliance with return processes through training and incentives
4. **Data Governance Implementation**
    o Established a governance structure with regional data stewards and system integration protocols
    o Enforced standards for data entry, exception reporting, and cross-system validation

Outcome

Through this transformation, the company established **greater confidence in its SPSCM data foundation**, allowing for:

- More proactive and accurate service parts planning
- Better SLA adherence across global markets
- Increased reuse of repairable parts
- Stronger customer relationships due to improved service continuity

Key Takeaway

- This use case demonstrates that **data integrity is not a back-office concern,** but a foundational requirement for executing an effective global SPSCM. Organizations must look beyond system functionality and prioritize **data integration, accessibility, and governance** to unlock the full potential of their SPSCM investments.

Conclusion: Data-Driven Excellence in SPSCM

In SPSCM, data is not just a tool—it is a critical enabler of operational success. From forecasting and procurement to field service and inventory management, every decision relies on high-quality, well-aligned, and timely data. Failure to manage data effectively results in missed SLAs, excess costs, customer dissatisfaction, and internal frustration.

To optimize SPSCM, organizations must prioritize:

- Investing in systems that not only collect but also contextualize data
- Enforcing strict data quality standards and governance
- Facilitating collaboration across departments to eliminate silos
- Upgrading integration to create real-time visibility across systems

Ultimately, the path to a more agile, cost-efficient, and customer-responsive SPSCM begins with one foundational principle: **trustworthy data powers everything**.

Chapter 13

Technology as the Backbone of SPSCM: Aligning Systems for Performance

Chapter Introduction:
Why Technology Compatibility Matters in SPSCM

In today's hyper-competitive service environment, technology serves as the central nervous system of SPSCM. It enables the coordination of complex networks, streamlines operations, and supports the real-time decision-making needed to meet aggressive SLAs. But as critical as technology is, its effectiveness hinges on interoperability and data alignment.

Unlike forward supply chains, where technology stacks often mature in predictable stages, the SPSCM ecosystem is built around reactive service models, a diverse product mix, and regionally fragmented infrastructure. This diversity puts significant pressure on legacy and modern technologies to interoperate—often across decades-old infrastructure, and siloed data systems.

The ability to maintain synchronization between systems like ERP, WMS, TMS, CRM, and dedicated SPSCM forecasting platforms is not just a technical convenience—it is a strategic imperative. Misaligned or poorly integrated systems can create data lags, inaccuracies, and blind spots that derail forecasting, slow repair cycles, inflate inventory buffers, and ultimately degrade customer satisfaction.

Expanded Core Content:
Technology Alignment in SPSCM

A Diverse Technology Landscape

SPSCM technology stacks typically include:

- **Customer Relationship Management (CRM):** Manages sales pipelines, customer service interactions, and installed base data. While not designed for logistics, CRM systems hold essential data (e.g., product entitlements, site locations) that can significantly improve service parts forecasting.

- **Enterprise Resource Planning (ERP):** The operational and financial nerve center. ERPs orchestrate procurement, order management, and supplier interaction—but regional configurations, regulatory customizations, and historical implementations can create incompatibility and reporting delays.
- **Warehouse Management Systems (WMS):** Facilitates real-time visibility of inventory levels, parts movements, and stock positions. These are often implemented per region and can lead to data fragmentation when not connected via a unified data strategy.
- **Transportation Management Systems (TMS):** Optimize the flow of parts between hubs, depots, and end-user locations. They help enforce SLA delivery windows but must be tightly integrated with service order systems to operate effectively.
- **Service Parts Forecasting and Planning Software:** This niche layer is central to SPSCM. It predicts future demand, sets stocking levels, and coordinates repair-versus-buy sourcing decisions. For this software to work correctly, it must continuously ingest accurate, current data from upstream systems like CRM and ERP.

SPSCM Technology & Data Stack

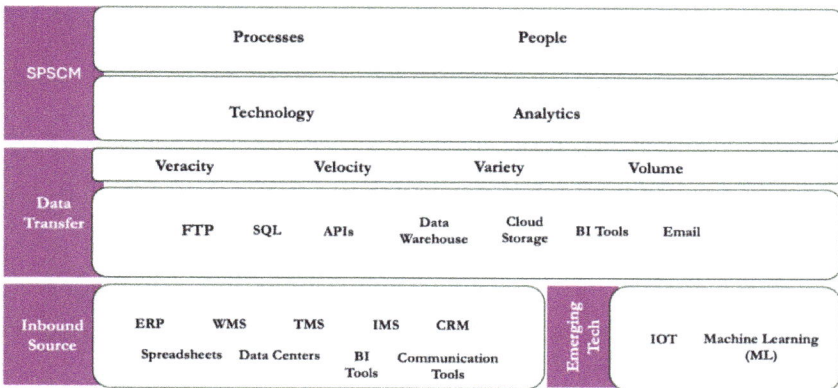

SPSCM		
	Processes	People
	Technology	Analytics

Data Transfer						
Veracity	Velocity		Variety		Volume	
FTP	SQL	APIs	Data Warehouse	Cloud Storage	BI Tools	Email

Inbound Source					Emerging Tech		
ERP	WMS	TMS	IMS	CRM		IOT	Machine Learning (ML)
Spreadsheets	Data Centers	BI Tools	Communication Tools				

**Technology-Driven Use Case:
System Alignment for Forecast Optimization**

A global electronics OEM was operating with siloed data across regions. The North American CRM system tracked entitlements, while the European platform lacked that capability. The ERP system had mismatched part definitions, and the WMS was using outdated stock classifications in Asia.

Because of these misalignments:

- Service part forecasts were inconsistent.
- Technicians were provided with incorrect entitlement information, impacting customer satisfaction.
- Regional planners had to pad inventory to compensate for poor data reliability.

By launching a global integration initiative—standardizing product codes, unifying CRM data, and synchronizing ERP-WMS transactions via APIs— they enabled accurate forecasting and real-time visibility across regions. The company saw a marked reduction in safety stock buffers, faster repair cycles, and improved SLA compliance.

Summary:
Why Technology Interoperability is Non-Negotiable

SPSCM is inherently cross-functional, spanning multiple geographies and product lines. Technology's role in this ecosystem is to unify fragmented data sources, streamline execution processes, and empower real-time decisions. But the presence of technology alone is not enough. True value is unlocked only when systems speak the same language, data flows seamlessly, and operational handoffs occur without friction.

Companies that treat technology compatibility as a strategic priority will gain a competitive advantage—not just in efficiency, but in agility and customer satisfaction. Those that fail to invest in harmonizing their tech stack will continue to suffer from inefficiencies, inflated costs, and frustrated customers and employees.

Use Case: Aligning Disparate Systems to Improve Global SPSCM Efficiency at a Medical Device Manufacturer

Background

A global medical device manufacturer supports hospitals and clinics across sixty-plus countries, supplying thousands of service parts for MRI machines, infusion pumps, and diagnostic tools. The company's SPSCM operations were suffering from recurring challenges, including:

- Regional stockouts despite healthy global inventory
- Inconsistent part availability data across regions
- Manual reconciliation of entitlements during service events
- Duplicate part forecasts across geographies

The root cause? A fragmented technology stack.

Technology Landscape

- **ERP Systems**: Two major platforms (SAP and Oracle) used by different regions due to prior acquisitions
- **CRM Systems**: North America used Salesforce with entitlement tracking; Europe used a legacy CRM with no visibility into the installed base
- **WMS**: Multiple regional instances without real-time connectivity
- **SPSCM Planning Software**: A specialized forecasting tool in place but fed by inconsistent upstream data from ERP and CRM systems
- **Field Service Systems**: Used for technician dispatch but not integrated with the CRM or WMS, resulting in service delays and misaligned part orders

Challenges

- **Data Inconsistency**: Part numbers, customer identifiers, and service level definitions varied between systems, leading to confusion and inefficiencies in forecasting and service execution.
- **Forecast Inaccuracy**: The planning software received inconsistent entitlement and failure rate data, reducing the precision of stocking algorithms.
- **Poor SLA Adherence**: Technicians frequently lacked correct part kits due to poor coordination between service orders and inventory systems.

- **High Inventory Buffers**: To hedge against uncertainty, regional planners carried excess safety stock, increasing working capital costs.

Solution

The company launched on a **Global SPSCM Technology Alignment Initiative** focused on five key steps:

- **Data Standardization**: Unified part numbering, customer identifiers, and entitlement definitions across all platforms
- **Integration via Middleware and APIs**: Connected ERP, CRM, WMS, and field service systems using modern APIs and a shared data hub
- **Real-time Syncing**: Enabled near real-time updates for key fields—stock levels, demand signals, and part failure rates
- **Entitlement Visibility Expansion**: Extended installed base visibility across all regions by replicating Salesforce functionality globally
- **Governance Model**: Created a cross-functional data governance team to maintain data consistency and resolve system misalignments

Results

- **Improved Forecasting Accuracy**: With consistent failure rate and entitlement data, the forecasting engine's accuracy increased, reducing understocking and overstocking.
- **Reduced Technician Delays**: Integrated systems ensured technicians had access to the correct parts with clear entitlement validation.
- **Lower Inventory Costs**: Harmonized stocking strategies across the network reduced unnecessary inventory buffers.
- **Faster Repair Cycles**: Improved system integration reduced order-to-ship cycle time for critical spares.

Key Takeaway

This use case highlights how **technology interoperability** and **system alignment** directly impact SPSCM efficiency, cost control, and service reliability. Organizations cannot rely on a variety of unconnected systems—only through seamless coordination across platforms can SPSCM deliver consistent, data-driven outcomes.

Chapter 14

Shared Ownership:
How Cross-Functional Alignment
Drives SPSCM Success

Setting the Context

In any organization that supports complex products post-sale, the SPSCM function is essential yet often misunderstood. Its unique combination of forecasting, logistics, planning, and inventory optimization spans the globe, supports mission-critical equipment, and responds to unpredictable service events—all while trying to meet financial and performance targets.

Despite its importance, SPSCM is often seen as an underperforming function. Leaders may view it as chaotic, slow-moving, or incapable of delivering consistent results. But beneath these surface perceptions lies a fundamental truth: **the effectiveness of the SPSCM is not determined by the SPSCM team alone**, it is largely shaped by the broader organizational environment in which it operates. From engineering to finance, field service to IT, nearly every department plays a role in either enabling or constraining the SPSCM's performance.

Cross-Functional Impacts on SPSCM: A Systemic View

1. Corporate Strategy: Setting the DNA of SPSCM

The overarching corporate strategy establishes the foundational constraints and opportunities for the SPSCM. Strategic decisions—such as entering new geographic markets, acquiring competitors, or maintaining legacy product support for extended periods—directly influence:

- **SPSCM model design** (e.g., OEM-based versus service provider networks)
- **Service part lifecycles** and long-term availability requirements
- **Customer commitments,** like uptime guarantees and support SLAs
- **System integration and technology investments**

In essence, the complexity and structure of the SPSCM network reflect the strategic commitments the company has made.

2. Sales & Marketing: Commitments Drive Complexity

Sales and marketing often introduce performance guarantees and product offerings that have deep implications for the SPSCM, such as:

- **Aggressive SLAs** that require inventory near the point of service
- **Multi-region or multi-product support contracts**
- **Under- or over-forecasted sales projections**
- **Sales incentives** that may encourage bundling or overselling of service contracts

These decisions impact inventory levels, warehouse design, staffing, and forecast accuracy, ultimately affecting SPSCM's ability to deliver.

3. Product Engineering: Design Determines Serviceability

Engineering decisions on how products are designed and assembled greatly influence the service supply chain's ability to respond effectively:

- **Serviceability and modularity** determine the complexity of field repair or part replacement.
- **Product reliability and MTBF** impact stocking strategies.
- **Service Parts BOM accuracy** ensures the right parts are available during early product rollout.
- **Part reuse or standardization** approaches to simplify the part sharing across product lines.

A design that is not service-friendly—however innovative—creates hidden downstream costs and inefficiencies in SPSCM operations.

4. Field Service Operations: Execution Impacts Inventory

Field service technicians are frontline contributors to the actual execution of the SPSCM. Their behavior affects:

- **Return rates for defective or unused parts**
- **Accuracy of failure reports**
- **Real-time part consumption visibility**
- **Avoidance of informal or unauthorized (shadow) stockpiling**

Lack of discipline in these areas can distort demand signals, inflate forecasts, and lead to inventory imbalances.

Influence on SPSCM Performance

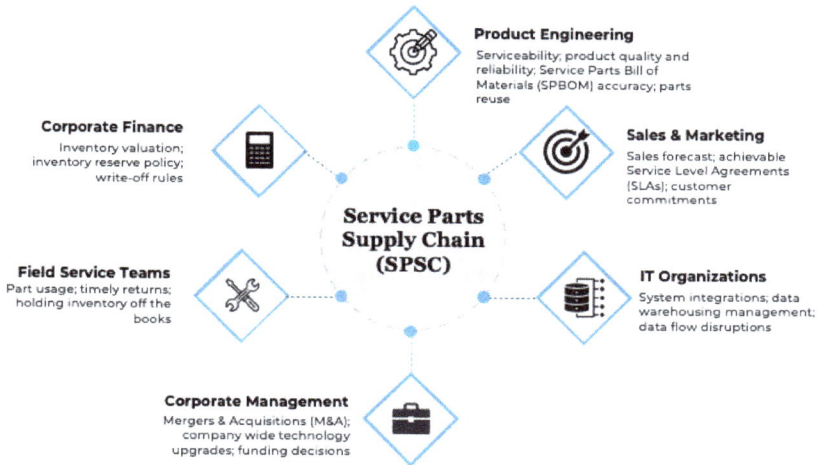

Product Engineering
Serviceability; product quality and reliability; Service Parts Bill of Materials (SPBOM) accuracy; parts reuse

Corporate Finance
Inventory valuation; inventory reserve policy; write-off rules

Sales & Marketing
Sales forecast; achievable Service Level Agreements (SLAs); customer commitments

Service Parts Supply Chain (SPSC)

Field Service Teams
Part usage; timely returns; holding inventory off the books

IT Organizations
System integrations; data warehousing management; data flow disruptions

Corporate Management
Mergers & Acquisitions (M&A); company wide technology upgrades; funding decisions

5. IT and Data Management: The Digital Backbone

The ability of SPSCM to function efficiently depends on how IT enables (or inhibits) the flow of clean, timely, and integrated data across systems:

- **Legacy systems and incompatible interfaces** often delay updates or create duplicate records.
- **Lack of advanced analytics and decision support tools** can impact planning and responsiveness.
- **System downtime or data latency** in ERP, CRM, and WMS platforms can severely disrupt operations.

When data is fragmented or slow, SPSCM performance drops—even if all other factors are optimized.

6. Finance: Policy Shapes Planning Behavior

Corporate finance plays a crucial role in inventory-related decisions by defining:

- **Excess and obsolete (E&O) policies**
- **Inventory valuation and write-down rules**
- **Capital allocation decision for inventory and repair center investments**
- **Risk tolerance for spare parts availability versus cost**

Chapter Summary: A Network of Influence

The SPSCM is a mirror that reflects the decisions made across the entire enterprise. Its structure, responsiveness, and efficiency are not determined in isolation—they are the cumulative output of choices made by strategic leaders, engineers, marketers, IT architects, field operators, and finance controllers.

To improve SPSCM performance, organizations must go beyond internal optimization and look outward, fostering alignment across all contributing functions. Without this integrated perspective, even the best SPSCM strategies will inevitably fall short.

Use Case: Elevating SPSCM Performance Through Cross-Functional Alignment at a Global Industrial Equipment Firm

Background

A global manufacturer of heavy industrial equipment supported a fleet of 10,000 machines operating in mining, energy, and construction sectors. Despite substantial investment in service operations, the company faced:

- Missed SLA targets for premium clients
- Excess inventory in North America and shortages in Asia
- Frequent friction between SPSCM and Field Service teams
- Inaccurate forecasts and underperforming repair centers

Problem Diagnosis

An internal audit revealed that the root causes were not isolated within the SPSCM team. They stemmed from disconnected decisions across the organization:

- **Engineering** had introduced three new equipment lines with no shared service BOM or reusable parts.
- **Sales** offered 24-hour uptime guarantees in Southeast Asia without involving the supply chain in the planning process.
- **Field Technicians** frequently retained unused parts in personal lockers, skewing demand visibility.
- **Finance** had implemented aggressive write-down policies that discouraged buffer stockholding.

- **IT** still operated two separate ERP instances post-merger, with no unified view of global inventory.

Solutions

The company launched a Service Parts Governance Council, pulling together leaders from SPSCM, Engineering, Sales, IT, and Finance. Together they implemented:

- A **cross-functional product launch checklist** to ensure SPBOM readiness
- **SLA feasibility reviews** before client contracts were finalized
- A **technician returns incentive program** to eliminate shadow inventories
- **Implemented unified ERP inventory views** and established consistent part naming conventions
- **Aligned financial KPIs between SPSCM and Finance** to support service-level investments

Outcome:

- **SLA compliance** improved in targeted regions.
- **Global inventory carrying cost** dropped without compromising service.
- **Field service productivity** due to improved parts availability and coordination.
- **New product launches** included SPSCM input from Day 1.

Chapter 15

Mergers & Acquisitions, and the Fragmentation Risk in SPSCM

Setting the Stage for Complexity

In today's competitive and innovation-driven economy, **mergers and acquisitions (M&A)** are routine strategies for growth, diversification, and market entry. For many companies, these transitions represent opportunity and scale—but for SPSCM, they often bring unprecedented levels of disruption. While executive teams focus on financial synergies or product portfolio expansion, SPSCM teams are left to untangle a web of incompatible technologies, conflicting service level agreements, inconsistent inventory policies, and fractured data landscapes.

Unlike production supply chains—which may be streamlined after integration—SPSCM is permanently impacted by legacy service obligations, decentralized inventories, and an installed base that can't simply be restructured. This chapter explores how M&A events affect SPSCM operations through the lens of external influence—particularly data, technology, and operational complexity—and offers strategies for navigating these transitions effectively.

The Hidden Complexities of M&A in SPSCM

Mergers and acquisitions introduce new dimensions to complexity in SPSCM, often amplifying existing challenges in demand planning, network design, and performance management. During post-M&A integration, several disruptions frequently emerge that demand careful attention.

One common disruption stems from conflicting service models and SLAs. Each acquired entity typically brings its own set of customer commitments, such as varying response time guarantees—ranging from four-hour service to next-business-day support—different warranty durations, and distinct service coverage standards. Additionally, some SLAs may be client-specific, further complicating their alignment with existing company policies. The result is a tangle of overlapping support obligations, excessive inventory held to meet incompatible targets, and confusion for planners and field service teams trying to interpret and honor diverse rules.

Another major complication is the expansion of service part complexity. M&A often introduces thousands of new service part numbers into the ecosystem, many of which may be redundant, serving the same function but labeled with different names or formats. SPBOM structures and product hierarchies can vary significantly, creating inconsistencies that planners must resolve. They must determine which parts are interchangeable, which obsolete components remain under active support contracts, and how to streamline duplication without compromising historical service obligations.

Further, M&A often leads to a more fragmented installed base and expanded network reach. Supporting new regions or geographies can disrupt previously optimized inventory networks. Existing hubs may no longer align with customer locations, and cross-border regulations or customs compliance introduce additional hurdles. This geographic expansion complicates inventory stocking strategies, lead-time management, and regulatory procedures for importing or exporting critical service parts.

While visible inventory and SLA challenges attract attention, underlying data and technology issues are often the root cause of persistent inefficiencies. M&A scenarios frequently result in the coexistence of multiple, disconnected ERP and WMS systems, along with CRM platforms from both entities—such as SAP versus Oracle or other competing technologies. This fragmentation creates duplicate data entries, conflicting part numbers, version mismatches, and a lack of real-time visibility into consolidated inventory or demand. Cross-functional workflows break down, replaced by error-prone manual workarounds.

Beyond the systems themselves, data model incompatibility also plays a significant role. Discrepancies in unit of measure (e.g., inches versus millimeters), different definitions for failure rates and MTBF, naming conventions, or part status codes undermine unified operation. Without harmonized data models, the merged SPSCM cannot accurately forecast, optimize inventory, track lifecycle stages, or monitor SLA compliance.

In many cases, full integration is delayed or avoided altogether, leaving companies in a "half-merged" state for years. This creates a fragmented decision-making environment in which teams rely on different data sources, adopt inconsistent processes, and experience delays due to disjointed approvals, fulfillment, and escalations. This dual-system condition severely limits scalability, operational accuracy, and service quality.

The operational impacts of M&A extend beyond IT and data. Supplier relationship disruptions are common, as sourcing contracts from each company must be renegotiated or terminated. Duplicate suppliers might exist yet consolidating them may introduce contractual risks. Lead times and pricing structures may shift unexpectedly, affecting part availability. Field service coordination also suffers; technicians may be trained on different tools and procedures, and decentralized warehousing contributes to fulfillment delays and part shortages. Effective knowledge sharing is hindered by incompatible systems and lack of shared workflows.

Finally, M&A often brings talent and organizational misalignment. Teams may differ culturally in their approach to planning, compliance, and escalation management. The loss of institutional knowledge through voluntary turnover post-acquisition weakens capabilities, while unclear roles and redundancies slow down decision-making. These operational misalignments are just as critical to address as technology and data issues, especially when aiming for seamless integration in a complex service parts environment.

M&A Impact Zones on SPSCM

SPSCM Zone	Pre-M&A State	M&A Shock (Post Acquisition)	Post-Integration Design
Technology Systems	Unified ERP, WMS, CRM tools with standard workflows	Multiple ERPs (e.g., SAP + Oracle), WMS incompatibility, siloed systems, no shared visibility	Consolidated tech stack, unified platforms, aligned processes, shared system access
Data & Master Records	Standardized parts catalog, BOM, MTBFs, lifecycle codes	Duplicate part numbers, mismatched BOMs, inconsistent failure rate data, incompatible units of measure	Harmonized data dictionary, master data governance, integrated lifecycle tracking
Service Level Agreements (SLAs)	Consistent SLAs across clients and products	Conflicting SLAs (e.g., four-hour versus NBD), unclear ownership, overcommitment to legacy clients	SLA harmonization, renegotiated contracts, tiered service levels aligned to new support model
Inventory Network	Optimized stocking locations, balanced safety stock	Redundant stocking locations, overstocking due to SLA confusion, lack of visibility across entities	Network redesign with merged demand profile, regional optimization, inventory pooling

SPSCM Zone	Pre-M&A State	M&A Shock (Post Acquisition)	Post-Integration Design
Supplier & Procurement	Unified contracts, volume-based pricing, preferred vendor list	Multiple contracts for same parts, vendor duplication, conflicting terms and pricing	Supplier consolidation, contract renegotiation, unified sourcing strategy
Field Service Operations	Standard tools, training, return processes	Technicians unfamiliar with new products, duplicated return depots, different training protocols	Cross-trained workforce, merged support documentation, unified reverse logistics
Forecasting & Planning	Reliable demand history and analytics pipeline	Fragmented data, misaligned forecasts, inconsistent part usage history	Integrated planning platform, aligned forecast models, shared planning assumptions
Customer Communication	Unified support messaging and customer experience	Mixed messages to customers, service delays, uncertainty on support rights	Consolidated customer portal, clear communication of merged service offerings
Compliance & Risk	Aligned financial controls, inventory policies, and quality systems	Conflicting audit rules, differing E&O policies, regional compliance mismatches	Unified risk controls, inventory valuation standards, audit-readiness planning

Closing Summary:
M&A Requires Deliberate SPSCM Integration

M&A can be a powerful growth driver, but for SPSCM teams, it introduces compounded complexity. Legacy obligations, system misalignment, and operational fragmentation can persist for years if integration is not deliberate, cross-functional, and well-resourced. SPSCM must be part of the **Day 1 planning discussion**, with dedicated tracks for data harmonization, SLA reconciliation, and inventory optimization. Only through early involvement, clear integration goals, and systemwide alignment can SPSCM transform from a liability into a value driver post-M&A.

The Hidden Complexities of M&A in SPSCM

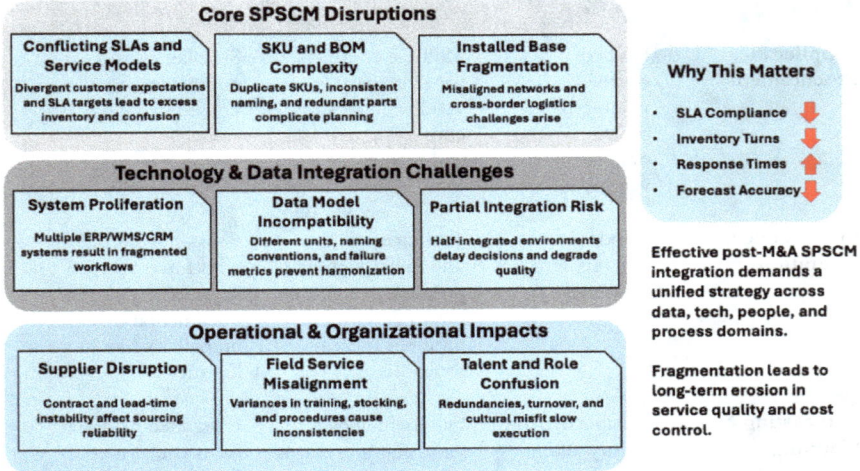

Core SPSCM Disruptions

Conflicting SLAs and Service Models
Divergent customer expectations and SLA targets lead to excess inventory and confusion

SKU and BOM Complexity
Duplicate SKUs, inconsistent naming, and redundant parts complicate planning

Installed Base Fragmentation
Misaligned networks and cross-border logistics challenges arise

Technology & Data Integration Challenges

System Proliferation
Multiple ERP/WMS/CRM systems result in fragmented workflows

Data Model Incompatibility
Different units, naming conventions, and failure metrics prevent harmonization

Partial Integration Risk
Half-integrated environments delay decisions and degrade quality

Operational & Organizational Impacts

Supplier Disruption
Contract and lead-time instability affect sourcing reliability

Field Service Misalignment
Variances in training, stocking, and procedures cause inconsistencies

Talent and Role Confusion
Redundancies, turnover, and cultural misfit slow execution

Why This Matters

- SLA Compliance ⬇
- Inventory Turns ⬇
- Response Times ⬆
- Forecast Accuracy ⬇

Effective post-M&A SPSCM integration demands a unified strategy across data, tech, people, and process domains.

Fragmentation leads to long-term erosion in service quality and cost control.

Use Case: M&A Disruption and Integration at a Global Networking Equipment Manufacturer

Background

A multinational technology firm acquired a competitor to expand its portfolio of enterprise networking products. The acquired company had a strong presence in Asia and supported its products with a regional service model very different from the acquirer's global centralized model.

Challenges Encountered

1. **Technology Misalignment:**
   o The two companies used incompatible ERP systems (SAP and NetSuite), resulting in fragmented inventory visibility.
   o Technicians had no access to the acquired company's service history or failure rates for installed base products.
2. **Conflicting SLAs:**
   o Legacy clients from the acquired firm expected same-day service, while the acquiring company offered next-business-day.
   o Support staff were unsure which commitments applied to merged accounts.

3. **Operational Redundancy:**
   - The inventory network had five redundant warehouses across Asia.
   - Both firms sourced from overlapping suppliers but had different contract terms.
4. **Field Service Inefficiencies:**
   - Field technicians were unsure which parts were compatible across product lines due to undocumented part equivalencies.
   - Knowledge systems were siloed—each team had separate troubleshooting documentation and no unified field portal.

Resolution and Integration Strategy

The company created a **SPSCM Integration Task Force** reporting to the executive steering committee, with mandates to:

- Consolidate ERP systems onto SAP within eighteen months.
- Develop a **Service BOM normalization strategy** to identify redundant SKUs.
- Rebuild the global inventory model using demand data from both companies.
- Harmonize SLAs through customer renegotiation and cross-training field teams.
- Merge supplier contracts under unified procurement to optimize costs and terms.

Results

- Inventory costs were reduced through warehouse consolidation.
- SLA compliance improved across the combined customer base.
- Forecast accuracy improved due to unified failure rate tracking and demand history consolidation.
- Customer satisfaction scores increased as service consistency was restored.

Section Summary:
Navigating Complexity Through Integration, Ownership, and Alignment

SPSCM is one of the most complex operational systems within any global enterprise. Its performance depends not on isolated actions, but on a deeply interconnected ecosystem where **data, technology, cross-functional ownership**, and **business continuity through M&A** each play a critical role.

Data is the lifeblood of SPSCM. It flows across systems and regions, enabling forecasting, inventory management, service responsiveness, and customer satisfaction. Yet, the quality of this data is only as good as the systems that capture, transmit, and interpret it. Disparities in lifecycle tracking, installed base accuracy, and failure rates directly translate to inefficiencies and cost. Therefore, governing data with a unified strategy is essential to creating a reliable, scalable SPSCM foundation.

Technology, meanwhile, is the nervous system of SPSCM operations. But few organizations possess a fully unified, modernized tech stack. Most are managing a hybrid of legacy and cloud systems, creating a fractured ecosystem. Achieving system compatibility and architectural alignment between platforms like ERP, CRM, WMS, TMS, and planning tools is not just a technical task—it is a strategic imperative. Misaligned systems generate delays, inconsistencies, and prevent the orchestration needed for high service performance.

The path to sustained SPSCM success also requires recognizing that **ownership is shared across the company**. SPSCM is shaped by corporate strategy, sales commitments, engineering design decisions, IT architecture, finance policy, and field service execution. Each of these groups contribute constraints—or enablers—that determine the service supply chain's potential. Cross-functional collaboration must therefore move from ad hoc communication to structured, ongoing engagement. Without shared ownership, even the most advanced tools or well-structured inventory networks will fall short.

Finally, **M&A** add another dimension of disruption. While they offer strategic growth opportunities, they also introduce redundant part numbers, conflicting SLAs, incompatible systems, and fragmented networks. SPSCM teams often inherit these complexities with little control over the pace or method of integration. Navigating M&A successfully requires proactive planning, early alignment with integration teams, and a roadmap that focuses on harmonizing systems, processes, and data standards across both legacy and new entities.

In conclusion, the SPSCM cannot be optimized in isolation. It reflects the broader organization—its history, its structure, and its ability to align. To elevate SPSCM performance, companies must invest in **integrated data, modern and compatible technology, shared cross-functional accountability**, and **resilient post-M&A strategies**. Only through this holistic lens can SPSCM evolve into a responsive, predictive, and value-generating function within the enterprise.

Part 4: Overview
Uncovering Optimization Opportunities

Up to this point, we have examined the defining characteristics that distinguish the service parts supply chain (SPSC), and its management framework (SPSCM) from the more traditional forward supply chain (FSC) and forward supply chain management (FSCM). We've also highlighted the significant challenges SPSCM faces—ranging from legacy obligations and fragmented networks to complex data landscapes and external influences—that contribute to its inherent complexity.

Now, in the final section of this book, our focus will transition from defining and diagnosing these complexities to identifying practical opportunities for optimization. This includes exploring how organizations can navigate these challenges and build both resilience and strategic advantage into the SPSCM framework.

In the pages ahead, we will explore:

The Five-Forces of SPSCM Operations

Chapter 16 will define a foundational principle called "**The Five-Forces of SPSCM Operations,**" in which we will explore the relationships among **Business Demands, Data, Technology, People,** and **Process**.

Approach to Uncovering the SPSCM Five-Forces

Chapter 17 will examine the underlying dynamics of SPSCM, focusing on what lies beneath the visible surface of the operation. This chapter will also introduce the **Five-Forces Assessment.** An approach that SPSCM organizations can use to gain a baseline understanding of why their operations function as they do—and to identify opportunities for improvement.

Chapter 16

The Five-Forces of SPSCM Operations

Defining the Five-Forces of SPSCM Operations

In previous chapters, we examined how SPSCM differs from traditional supply chains and explored the specific challenges it faces—ranging from unpredictable demand patterns to geographic complexity and high service level expectations. Now we shift from diagnosing the "what" and the "why" of SPSCM challenges to understanding the foundation of "how" behind the operation.

In this chapter, we will introduce a comprehensive model that defines the key drivers of SPSCM performance: the **Five-Forces of SPSCM Operations**. These forces are not just academic concepts—they are the operational levers that determine how effectively a service supply chain can respond to customer demands, deliver parts on time, and remain cost-effective across complex, often global, networks.

In this chapter, will cover:

- **The Five-Forces of SPSCM Operations**:
    - **Business Demands** – the origins of SPSCM strategy and pressures
    - **Data** – the source of visibility, accuracy, and planning integrity
    - **Technology** – the infrastructure that enables flow and execution
    - **People** – the operators, interpreters, and orchestrators of the system
    - **Process** – the output of all other forces, translated into actions
- A **detailed breakdown** of each force, including:
    - Their characteristics and roles
    - How they interact with each other
    - Their influence on operational performance and constraints

The Five-Forces Analogy:
SPSCM as a Gearbox Assembly

To visualize the interplay between these forces, imagine an automobile's motor drive system:

o   **The Engine = Business Demand**: Just as an engine powers the car, business demands (SLAs, product support requirements, market pressure) drive all SPSCM activity.

o   **The Transmission = Data, Technology, and People**: These forces act like the transmission gears, converting raw engine power into controlled motion. The better these gears mesh, the smoother the operation.

o   **The Gear Ratio = Operational Balance**: Each company's specific configuration of data quality, tech maturity, and human expertise creates a "gear ratio" that determines how well the SPSCM translates business demands into action.

o   **The Drive Wheels = Process Execution**: The efficiency of the wheels turning reflects the operational balance of the transmission, enabling execution of the business, planning, forecasting, fulfillment, returns, repair logistics, and inventory management.

The Five-Forces of SPSCM Operations

Business Demands
* Model Complexity
* Product Type
* SLA requirements

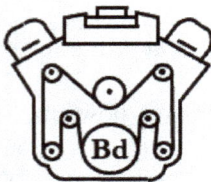

Technology
* Available & Present
* Legacy Mix
* Global Alignment

Data
* Available & Complete
* Understood & Representative
* Globally Aligned

People
* Skillset & Experience
* Regional Variances
* Proactive versus Reactive

Process
* Unique execution footprint
* Output from the relationships between data, technology & process.

Together, these forces shape the rhythm and responsiveness of SPSCM. Just like a high-performance car depends on the right balance between horsepower, transmission tuning, and traction, an effective SPSCM depends on the synergy between demand, enablement, and execution.

Why These Five-Forces Matter in SPSCM

SPSCM environments are rarely one-size-fits-all. Even within the same industry, different companies may use entirely different models based on the maturity and relationship of their Five-Forces. These relationships evolve over time and vary across regions, product lines, and business units.

For example:

- A company with strong automation but weak data governance may experience digital inefficiency—fast systems fed with poor input.
- An organization with rich data and talented people may perform well even with legacy systems—but will struggle to scale.
- Businesses with misaligned SLAs and processes (especially after mergers) often have internal conflicts between demand and operational reality.

Recognizing these force dynamics is essential for any company looking to transform its SPSCM. Instead of treating inefficiencies as isolated problems, organizations must evaluate their Five-Forces alignment holistically—like tuning an engine and transmission together rather than replacing just one part.

Use Case: Applying the Five-Forces in a High-Tech SPSCM

Consider a global electronics manufacturer supporting mission-critical hardware for the semiconductor industry. The business operates under tight service level agreements requiring parts deliveries within four hours in some geographies.

- **Business Demands are high:** Strict SLAs, low tolerance for downtime, and a globally distributed customer base

- **Data is partial:** Some regions have full installed base visibility, while others lack real-time failure reporting.

- **Technology is uneven:** Advanced routing and planning tools exist at headquarters, but local warehouses still rely on spreadsheets.

- **People** are skilled but stretched thin, especially in regions requiring manual intervention.

- **Processes are inconsistent:** Fulfillment is automated in some areas and entirely manual in others.

> **The results?** The company must dynamically rebalance its Five-Forces. In regions with weaker tech, they scale up human oversight and flexible processes. In high-tech regions, they rely on automation and centralized planning. The company's operational "gear ratio" shifts with its environment—revealing how the Five-Forces model can adapt to optimize outcomes under constraints.

Summary and Transition to Forces Breakdown

The Five-Forces model provides a powerful framework for analyzing, diagnosing, and improving SPSCM operations. Unlike linear supply chains, SPSCM operates with unique characteristics that depend on the dynamic interaction of demand, enablers, and execution.

In the next section, we will break down each of the Five-Forces individually, exploring their attributes, operational implications, and role in shaping overall performance. Whether you're designing a new SPSCM or optimizing an existing one, this breakdown will help you understand where to focus, what to improve, and how to realign the gears for maximum output unique to your operating model.

Breaking Down the Five-Forces Model

In the remainder of this chapter, we will explore each of the Five-Forces that shape the operational execution of SPSCM. Each force—**Business Demand, Data, Technology, People,** and **Process**—has unique characteristics, interdependencies, and a distinct influence on performance. Together, they form the operational architecture that determines how effectively an SPSCM can meet its goals.

Let's begin with Business Demands—the engine that starts it all.

Force #1: Business Demands – The Engine of SPSCM

Introduction

Business demands are the originating force in SPSCM—everything else follows their lead. These demands represent the strategic, operational, and market-facing requirements placed on the supply chain by the broader business. They define **what** must be delivered, **where**, and **how fast**, setting the tone for complexity, risk, and cost across the entire SPSCM landscape.

Returning to the drivetrain analogy introduced earlier, business demands are equivalent to the **engine assembly** of a vehicle. The engine defines the car's power, speed, and fuel consumption—just as business requirements define the size, scale, and responsiveness that the SPSCM must achieve. Whether you're supporting a mission-critical server or a low-cost consumer device, the power required by the business must be efficiently converted into execution.

Key Business Demand Drivers in SPSCM

Business demands come from both **product characteristics** and **organization structure**. Examples include:

- **Complex and extensive service parts BOMs (SPBOMs)**
  Products, with many serviceable components—often in the thousands—require granular inventory segmentation and planning across regions and time zones.
- **Quality and reliability issues**
  High failure rates lead to increased service incidents, forcing SPSCM to carry additional safety stock and accelerate logistics capabilities.
- **Geographic dispersion of the installed base**
  Global or remote customers require a wide-reaching network of parts locations or regionalized fulfillment centers, adding cost and coordination complexity.
- **Warranties, SLAs, and service contract obligations**
  The stricter the performance guarantees (e.g., four-hour part delivery), the more aggressive the SPSCM configuration must be—often trading efficiency for responsiveness.
- **Mergers, acquisitions, and product portfolio expansion**
  Each newly acquired business brings with it its own SPBOMs, installed base, and customer expectations, which must be integrated into the existing SPSCM architecture.

These variables directly influence the "load" that the SPSCM must carry—similar to an engine tuned for different driving conditions. High-torque engines (high-demand SPSCMs) require more advanced transmissions (data, technology, and people) to handle the strain without performance loss.

External Ownership of Business Demands

Business demands are typically shaped by **functions outside of SPSCM—**

product management, customer support, finance, engineering, and regional operations. These stakeholders may define requirements without understanding the operational consequences, which means SPSCM must constantly adapt to **external pressure** and **competing priorities**. This shared ownership dynamic often creates tension, as decisions made upstream cascade into significant cost and performance trade-offs downstream.

Impact of Product and Market Characteristics

The nature of the product being supported—its unique environment, reliability, and installation model—plays a major role in shaping demand. Consider the following scenarios:

- **Centralized Repair**
  For model or module products, centralized repair models can reduce inventory complexity by pooling risk.
- **Field Repair/Multi-Echelon Network**
  For fixed and complex assets (like medical imaging systems or semiconductor tools), distributed inventory across multiple echelons is required to support field technicians and local repairs. This increases both inventory and planning complexity.
- **Unreliable Products**
  When failure rates are high or unpredictable, the business demand creates urgency. SPSCM must absorb this volatility by maintaining higher stocking levels, which increases working capital and storage costs while elevating service delivery risk.
- **Remote Installation + Aggressive SLAs**
  This combination represents one of the most difficult SPSCM environments, where lead time compression and low predictability create a high risk of service failures, no matter how well inventory is planned.

M&A Complexity as a Business Demand Modifier

Mergers and acquisitions can significantly alter business demands overnight. Integrating multiple SPSCMs with different operational models is akin to **replacing an engine with a completely different design**, while expecting the same transmission and wheels to function seamlessly. New service commitments, parts portfolios, and support structures flood the system with unfamiliar requirements, often outpacing the organization's ability to adapt its supporting forces.

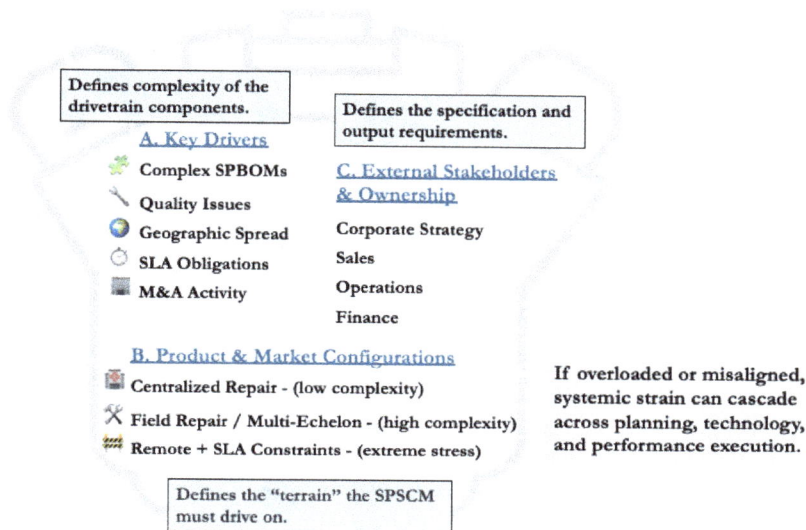

Even in the absence of an M&A, new product introductions act similarly, placing fresh and unfamiliar stress on existing systems. Unfortunately, unlike forward manufacturing, SPSCM infrastructure is difficult to retool once established. Warehouses, IT systems, vendor agreements, and staffing models do not pivot quickly. The business may change overnight; the SPSCM cannot.

Summary: Translating Business Demands into Execution

In summary, **Business Demands** form the starting point of all SPSCM action. They are the upstream forces that other components must respond to. Whether these demands are defined by product complexity, customer expectations, or structural changes such as M&A, their effect is always felt downstream in the form of urgency, complexity, and resource strain.

However, these demands do not directly power execution. Instead, they are converted into operational output by the **transmission system** of SPSCM: **Data, Technology,** and **People**. If these enablers are not aligned or properly configured, the power from the business engine may be lost, delayed, or misapplied—resulting in poor performance, high cost, or service failure.

In the next section, we will examine the first of these enablers: Data—the lifeblood of all SPSCM planning, execution, and insight.

Force #2: Data – Characteristics and Complexities

Introduction

If **Business Demands** are the engine driving SPSCM, then **Data** is the driving gear in the transmission that powers technology and people. Without high-quality, timely, and relevant data, even the most advanced planning systems or technologies will falter. In Chapter 12, we discussed how SPSCM operations are intensely data-dependent—and uniquely burdened by the four **V's of Big Data:** *Volume, Velocity, Variety,* and *Veracity*. These four attributes are particularly challenging in SPSCM, where real-time operational decisions must be made with imperfect or inconsistent data.

SPSCM doesn't operate on theory—it operates on data. But the real question is: *Is that data trustworthy, accurate, and reflective of reality?* The answer, too often, is *no*. And when the data is wrong, everything downstream—forecasts, inventory decisions, technology performance, and even labor processes—is compromised.

The Critical Role of Data in SPSCM

Data in SPSCM originates from an array of sources: field operations, installed base activity, part movements, customer transactions, supplier interactions, and external systems like 3PLs or IoT sensors. These sources feed into planning engines, forecasting tools, and inventory models—each relying on clean, structured, and accurate data to function.

However, real-world SPSCM data is rarely clean. It is often fragmented, duplicated, outdated, or misrepresented due to manual workarounds or system limitations. As a result, **technology becomes inefficient, human intervention increases,** and **processes are forced to absorb the inconsistency**—leading to overall degradation in operational performance.

Example: The Challenge of Demand Data Accuracy

Consider a company using an advanced forecasting and planning engine to manage a multi-echelon inventory network. This engine ingests usage data from various enterprise systems—MRP, ERP, and inventory platforms—to forecast future part demand across regional and global distribution centers.

However, the way this demand data is handled introduces several challenges:

- **Manual Adjustments Create Inconsistency**
  In some regions, large MRO-related replenishment spikes are manually removed from the data set, while in other regions, no such filtering is applied. This inconsistency distorts forecasting outputs.
- **Returns Cause Demand Inflation**
  Parts that are ordered but ultimately returned unused may not be properly adjusted out of the demand stream especially when returns occur after a cutoff date—leading to false signal of consumption.
- **Legacy Systems Obscure Substitution Chains**
  Regions using older MRP systems may not support tracking of part revisions or substitutions (part chaining), resulting in skewed forecasts for upgraded or newer replacement parts.

These issues illustrate a common truth: **the data that drives SPSCM decisions often doesn't accurately reflect operational reality**. This disconnect can lead to misallocated inventory, service failures, and excess costs. When asked how demand data is cleaned and audited, many organizations either lack a clear answer or admit the process is ad hoc, manual, and rarely reviewed.

Data Integrity and Transformation

SPSCM data is not static—it is transformed, restructured, filtered, and sometimes manipulated to suit system requirements or management needs. But in this transformation process, **context can be lost**, and **biases can be introduced**. For example:

> Removing a demand spike may be intended to normalize outliers. But if that spike was caused by a systemic product failure or latent defect, excluding it can lead to understocking and future service failures.

This dilemma—**is the data truly representative of what it intends to capture?**—is at the heart of SPSCM complexity.

In practice, SPSCM professionals must deal with:

- Inconsistent data formatting across systems
- Non-standard part naming conventions
- Disparate update frequencies
- Gaps in master data management
- Heavy use of Microsoft Excel as a shadow planning system

These are not theoretical issues; they manifest daily in operational firefighting, poor forecast accuracy, and planning inefficiencies.

Data – The Enabler Gear

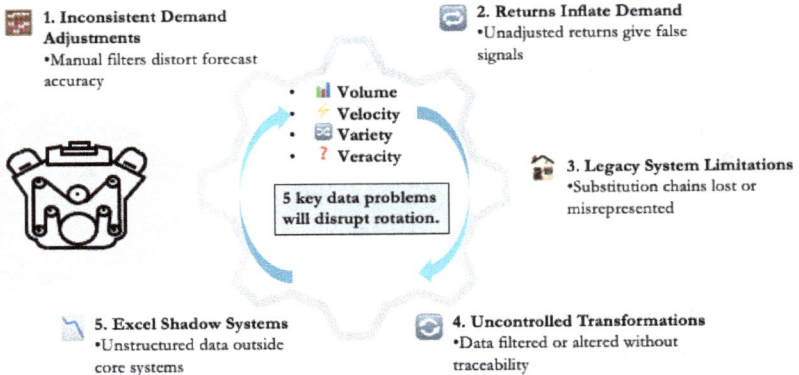

1. Inconsistent Demand Adjustments
•Manual filters distort forecast accuracy

2. Returns Inflate Demand
•Unadjusted returns give false signals

• **Volume**
• **Velocity**
• **Variety**
• **? Veracity**

5 key data problems will disrupt rotation.

3. Legacy System Limitations
•Substitution chains lost or misrepresented

5. Excel Shadow Systems
•Unstructured data outside core systems

4. Uncontrolled Transformations
•Data filtered or altered without traceability

Consequences of Poor Data Quality

When data lacks integrity or structure, it introduces friction across all SPSCM functions:

- **Technology malfunctions**: Planning engines make incorrect recommendations or require constant overrides.
- **Human labor increases**: Analysts and planners must clean, verify, and adjust data manually.
- **Process efficiency drops**: Workflows are disrupted, and service levels suffer.
- **Cost and risk increase**: Excess inventory is held to buffer against uncertainty, and service failures become more frequent.

Put simply: **data quality is not an IT problem—it is a core operational performance issue**.

Data Origin and Ecosystem Complexity

Data used in SPSCM originates from a wide range of sources with varying levels of accuracy and structure:

- Manually managed Excel spreadsheets
- IoT sensors tracking parts usage and failure rates

- Partner systems (e.g., 3PL logistics updates or supplier inventory feeds)
- Internal enterprise applications with different update cycles and data governance practices

Understanding these origins—and the reliability of each—is critical. Organizations must not only collect data but also **validate, transform, and contextualize it** for effective use. Data governance is not just a back-office function; it is the foundation upon which accurate decision-making in SPSCM is built.

Summary: Data as the Enabler and Limiter of SPSCM

In summary, Data is the foundational enabler—or limiter—of SPSCM performance. It directly affects the ability of systems, people, and processes to deliver results. Dirty data leads to faulty execution. Accurate, contextualized data enables smarter, faster decisions.

Yet, data is not necessarily useful on its own. It must be activated and processed through systems that understand its structure and purpose. This leads us to the next force in the model: Technology—the means by which data is converted into action across the SPSCM landscape.

Force #3: Technology – Capabilities and Limitations

Introduction

In SPSCM, **technology acts as the enabler of operational scale and efficiency,** converting data into actionable insights, coordinating inventory across networks, and driving automation across complex workflows. However, technology is not a standalone solution. It is inextricably linked to data quality, system integration, and organizational readiness.

If we could diagram a typical SPSCM operation, it would reveal a tangled web of interconnected systems—forecasting tools, ERP modules, inventory systems, CRM platforms—all exchanging data across generations of infrastructure. Much of this digital fabric has evolved over decades, built layer by layer with bolt-on solutions, manual processes, and semi-integrated tools.

This **interdependency of data and technology forms the digital backbone** of an SPSCM operation. Its strength—or fragility—directly influences efficiency, agility, and the ability to scale.

The Fragmented Technology Landscape in SPSCM

Today, most SPSCM operations sit atop a hybrid environment of technologies—some decades old, others newly cloud-based. The mix is rarely intentional; it reflects years of business changes, acquisitions, regional adaptations, and cost constraints. As a result:

- **Data integration is fragmented**: Information must be pulled, transformed, and manually reconciled across systems.

- **Workflows are inconsistent**: Teams adapt processes to accommodate system limitations or outdated tools.

- **Automation is limited**: Many functions still rely on spreadsheets or manual triggers to bridge technology gaps.

Technology – The Most Rigid and Least Adaptable Gear

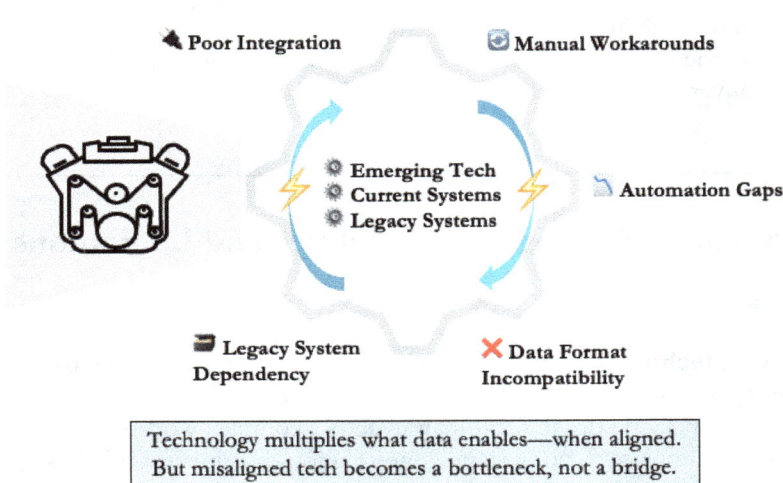

Poor Integration

Manual Workarounds

Emerging Tech
Current Systems
Legacy Systems

Automation Gaps

Legacy System Dependency

Data Format Incompatibility

Technology multiplies what data enables—when aligned. But misaligned tech becomes a bottleneck, not a bridge.

The result? **Technology implementations rarely meet expectations.** Companies invest in modern solutions assuming significant performance gains, but these gains are often eroded by:

- Incomplete data pipelines
- Poor master data governance
- System incompatibilities
- Underdeveloped user adoption

Technology Implementation: The Reality versus the Promise

Enterprise technology operates within a strict logic: it requires clean inputs, follows structured rules, and delivers outputs based on predefined configurations. But SPSCM is inherently unstructured, and exception-driven.

Some common limitations in practice:

- **Rigid input requirements**: Systems fail when upstream data isn't formatted or validated correctly.

- **Inflexible processes**: Software cannot easily adapt to real-world variability without costly customizations.

- **Unstructured edge cases**: About 30-40% of SPSCM workflows are not easily modeled in standard ERP or planning tools, leading to workarounds.

Business processes inefficiency and workarounds start to creep back into an operations post technology implementation

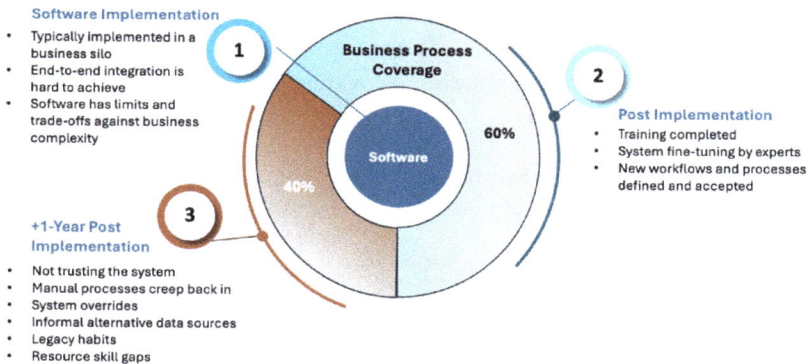

Software Implementation
- Typically implemented in a business silo
- End-to-end integration is hard to achieve
- Software has limits and trade-offs against business complexity

Post Implementation
- Training completed
- System fine-tuning by experts
- New workflows and processes defined and accepted

+1-Year Post Implementation
- Not trusting the system
- Manual processes creep back in
- System overrides
- Informal alternative data sources
- Legacy habits
- Resource skill gaps

Business Process Coverage

Software 60%

40%

These gaps eventually wear down system credibility. In many organizations, manual intervention creeps back in. Teams revert to Excel or bypass system logic altogether, undermining the very purpose of the technology investment.

A Legacy Burden: Technology Generations Collide

Older companies face a unique challenge: **decades of layered systems**, each capturing part of the operational picture. For example:

- A 1980s WMS that manages inbound warehouse receipts
- A 1990s MRP engine that calculates reorder points

- A 2000s Excel tool used for part substitution logic
- A modern SaaS platform introduced to standardize planning—but unable to access the above without heavy integration work.

Each new solution must be reconciled with existing architecture. Point-to-point connections may be created as stopgaps, but they only increase long-term complexity and maintenance cost.

The Emerging Frontier: Machine Learning and AI in SPSCM

Newer technologies like Machine Learning (ML) and Artificial Intelligence (AI) offer enormous potential for SPSCM, particularly in areas such as:

- Predictive failure analysis
- Real-time inventory optimization
- Dynamic safety stock recalculation
- Automated root-cause analysis for service issues

However, there is a catch: **ML and AI are only as powerful as the data behind them**. Most SPSCM environments are not yet prepared:

- Historical data is fragmented or missing.
- Data models are not structured for training purposes.
- System interoperability issues block real-time analysis.

Without foundational cleanup and integration, these innovations risk repeating the same pattern—high expectations, followed by partial or failed adoption.

Summary: Technology as a Force Multiplier or Constraint

Technology in SPSCM is not just an enabler—it is a **force multiplier** when executed well and a **bottleneck** when misaligned. Its effectiveness depends not only on the software itself but also on the quality of data it receives, the maturity of adjacent systems, and the people who operate it.

When technology works in harmony with data and people, it becomes a powerful engine for operational excellence. But when it is layered atop legacy systems without full integration or strategic alignment, it leads to inefficiencies, frustration, and a cycle of underperformance.

This leads us to the next force in the model: **People**—the human side of SPSCM. Technology can automate processes and scale decisions, but it is people who interpret, manage, and adapt those systems to real-world complexity. Understanding the role of workforce capabilities, organizational structure, and change management is essential to completing the picture of SPSCM performance.

People – Their Role and Impact in SPSCM

In SPSCM, no matter how advanced the technology or how refined the data, people remain the essential force that makes the operation function. Across every SPSCM organization, I've reviewed or audited—whether global enterprises or regional hubs—one constant holds true: the resilience, adaptability, and expertise of the people behind the scenes determine operational success.

Within the Five-Forces framework, people serve as the dynamic link between static technologies and rigid data architectures, enabling real-time decisions, managing exceptions, and ensuring continuity across complex networks. They are not just operators of systems—they are interpreters of nuance, solvers of breakdowns, and enablers of strategic agility.

The Human Backbone of SPSCM Operations

A high-performing SPSCM operation is typically staffed by professional with deep institutional knowledge and hard-earned experience. These individuals have often developed their expertise over years—sometimes decades— navigating complex operational environments and learning to anticipate challenges before they arise. Their intuitive understanding of product behavior, customer urgency, and supply constraints enables them to make decisions that no system, however sophisticated, can replicate.

However, these same experts often develop strong preferences for familiar workarounds and manual processes—tools born out of necessity to fill gaps in flawed systems or inconsistent data. While such behaviors may appear resistant to change, they are often rooted in a survival mindset: when systems fall short, people step in.

People – The Adaptive Gear

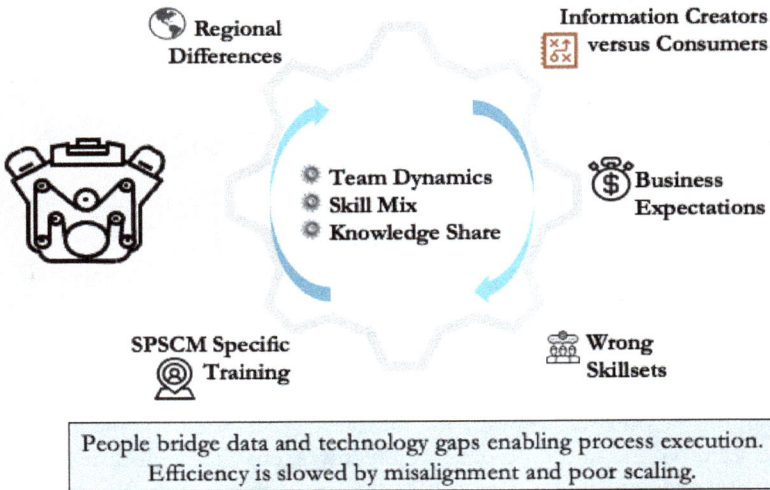

🌐 **Regional Differences**

Information Creators versus Consumers

⚙ **Team Dynamics**
⚙ **Skill Mix**
⚙ **Knowledge Share**

💰 **Business Expectations**

SPSCM Specific Training

Wrong Skillsets

People bridge data and technology gaps enabling process execution. Efficiency is slowed by misalignment and poor scaling.

The Misguided Expectation of Technology-Driven Headcount Reduction

Organizations frequently view new technology implementations as an opportunity to reduce workforce costs. The logic seems sound: better systems should mean fewer people. However, SPSCM is rarely so straightforward. The speculative, nonlinear, and exception-heavy nature of service parts supply chains demands human oversight, intervention, and judgment.

Premature headcount reductions can cripple SPSCM performance. While short-term savings may appear on the balance sheet, the long-term erosion of operational capability often goes unnoticed—until customer satisfaction drops, inventory write-offs climb, and service-level commitments falter. In fact, people often serve as the **adjustable gear** in the SPSCM drivetrain, compensating for inflexible systems and imperfect data. Reducing that adaptability weakens the entire system.

The Hidden Cost of Underestimating Human Capital

In many organizations, personnel expenses are viewed as variable costs—adjustable levers in response to financial pressure. Meanwhile, investments in software and infrastructure are often treated as sunk or fixed costs. This mindset leads to an imbalance: when performance fails to meet expectations, leadership often cuts staff rather than reassessing systemic gaps in tools or strategy.

Yet, the long lifecycle of service parts means that poor decisions today may not reveal their consequences for years. Over time, performance quietly deteriorates as institutional knowledge is lost and fewer hands remain to manage increasingly complex operations.

Instead of defaulting to cuts, organizations should reevaluate whether they have the **right mix of skills**. Optimizing the skill set—not just the size—of the workforce often yields more sustainable efficiency gains than blanket reductions.

Evolving the SPSCM Talent Profile

As SPSCM operations grow more data-intensive and technologically fragmented, specialized roles are increasingly necessary to maintain effectiveness. Two critical but often underrepresented roles include:

1. Data Management Specialists – Translating Operational Needs into Data Solutions

These professionals act as the connective tissue between operations and IT, ensuring that data is structured, integrated, and usable across systems. Their core responsibilities include:

- Mapping and transforming SPSCM data across legacy and modern platforms
- Maintaining data quality, consistency, and integrity
- Managing and auditing system inputs and outputs to reflect business intent

**Data Management Specialists
The Librarian of Data Management**

2. Data Scientists – Driving Predictive Insights and Innovation

These individuals apply analytics, machine learning, and statistical techniques to unlock insights from historical and real-time data. Their work enhances:

- Forecasting accuracy
- Risk modeling and mitigation
- Strategic inventory and network optimization
- Implementing AI and ML models

Data Scientists
The Detectives for Data Analysis and
Predictive Modeling

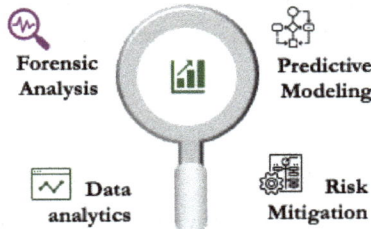

Forensic Analysis

Predictive Modeling

Data analytics

Risk Mitigation

It's essential to distinguish these roles. **Data management** focuses on making data available and reliable; **Data Scientists** transform that data into decision intelligence. Both are vital, but their success depends on proper alignment with SPSCM—not generic IT support. To ensure relevance and accountability, these roles should sit within (or report directly to) the SPSCM organization.

Organizational Design: Think Locally, Act Globally

Most SPSCM teams are structured regionally, reflecting the operational diversity of different geographies. Local leadership makes sense in managing region-specific service demands, cultural expectations, and regulatory requirements. However, regional silos can hinder global visibility, standardization, and inventory optimization.

To reconcile these tensions, global SPSCM functions should maintain **dotted-line reporting** or **matrixed authority** over regional teams. This allows:

- Consistent application of global best practices

- Centralized oversight of critical KPIs, like inventory turns and service levels
- Greater control over stocking strategies and transfer flows across regions

This hybrid structure maintains local agility while fostering global coherence—especially critical in long-lifecycle parts environments where every node in the supply chain affects overall performance.

Summary: People as the Linchpin of Performance

In the Five-Forces model, people represent the most adaptable and responsive element in SPSCM operations. Unlike technology or data—both of which are constrained by design—people provide the flexibility and judgment required to keep the operation functioning. They fill in the gaps, compensate for system limitations, and enable performance continuity in the face of uncertainty.

Underinvestment in people—whether through attrition, misaligned skillsets, or misguided cost-cutting—can quietly undermine the effectiveness of even the best-designed SPSCM frameworks.

As we now transition to the next force—**Process**—we explore how the routines, workflows, and decision-making structures used in SPSCM operations reinforce or hinder this human adaptability, and how mature processes can either empower or encumber the workforce that drives the business forward.

Processes – Definitions and Operational Modes in SPSCM

The fifth and final force in the Five-Forces model—**Process**—brings structure, discipline, and repeatability to the complexity of SPSCM. If business demand is the engine, and data, technology, and people are the transmission—operating at their own unique gear ratio—then process is the wheels that transfer output to the road. It keeps the car steady and absorbs power from the drivetrain. In essence, its ability to maintain control is driven by the composition and grip of the tires.

Processes dictate how inputs from people, data, and technology are orchestrated to produce consistent, auditable, and efficient operational outcomes. They transform reactive activities into intentional workflows and are essential for scalability, training, quality assurance, and performance measurement.

In SPSCM, where unpredictability, part variety, and lifecycle length create constant turbulence, **processes serve as stabilizers**. But these processes are not all created equal. They operate across a spectrum of visibility, maturity, and intent—and they can either enable agility or entrench dysfunction.

Categories of SPSCM Processes

SPSCM processes generally fall into **three distinct categories**, each with a unique role and set of risks.

1. Technology-Based Execution Processes

These are system-triggered processes, typically governed by preconfigured logic and business rules. They represent the most visible and auditable layer of operations.

Examples include:

- Executing purchase orders from a system-generated work queue
- Updating installed base records to reflect field asset changes
- Adjusting yield rates in inventory planning based on observed failure patterns
- Revising supplier lead times based on system feedback loops
- Responding to exception alerts from control towers or monitoring tools

These processes are efficient and scalable, but their effectiveness hinges on **data integrity and system configuration**. When data is flawed or the logic outdated, the processes fail silently, leading to recurring issues masked by automation.

2. Operational (Manual) Processes

These fill the gaps that technology hasn't solved. Often supported by **tacit knowledge**—know-how that comes from experience and practice, rather than being explicitly stated—and spreadsheets, these processes require human interpretation, decision-making, and judgment.

Examples include:

- Setting initial stocking levels for new or low-volume parts

- Forecasting last-time-buy (LTB) quantities for parts approaching obsolescence
- Creating failure-rate assumptions or chaining logic for product families
- Managing supersession logic when part hierarchies shift

While necessary, these processes are **prone to variation and error**—especially when undocumented or inconsistently applied across regions or teams. Their success depends heavily on the people performing them and their understanding of broader supply chain goals.

3. Hidden or Informal Processes

These are the "underground" processes that evolve organically within teams. They are rarely documented, often invisible to leadership, and almost never audited—yet they are **vital for daily execution**.

Examples include:

- Overriding system-calculated stocking levels based on field feedback or past experience
- Adjusting demand inputs to influence system outputs
- Creating custom spreadsheets to handle defective part returns, warranty exceptions, or vendor follow-ups

Hidden processes typically emerge from **mistrust in system outputs**, lack of process ownership, or poor integration across tools. While they can drive short-term effectiveness, they often introduce long-term risk, inconsistency, and dependency on individual expertise.

Rather than dismissing these informal processes, organizations should seek to identify, understand, and, where appropriate, formalize, or eliminate them—closing the gap between system design and operational reality.

The Influence of Regional Process Variation

SPSCM processes are rarely globally uniform. Over time, **regional operations develop their own adaptations**, driven by unique business environments, regulatory constraints, and cultural norms.

These variations often result in **fragmented systems and inconsistent practices** that hinder global visibility and performance comparison. Addressing these challenges requires **process harmonization**, where a core set of global standards is enforced while allowing controlled flexibility for regional compliance.

Regional Variances

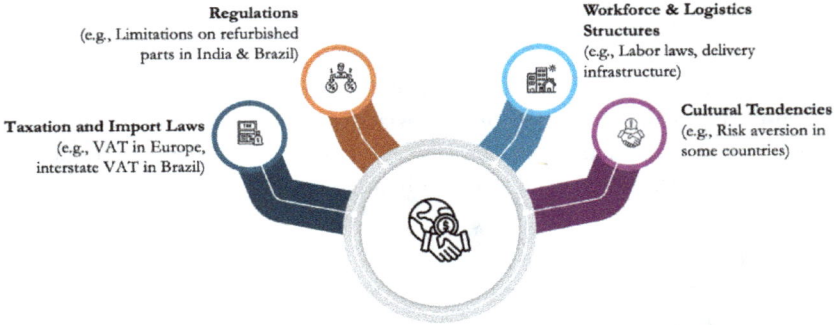

Regulations
(e.g., Limitations on refurbished parts in India & Brazil)

Workforce & Logistics Structures
(e.g., Labor laws, delivery infrastructure)

Taxation and Import Laws
(e.g., VAT in Europe, interstate VAT in Brazil)

Cultural Tendencies
(e.g., Risk aversion in some countries)

Summary: Process as the Enabler of Repeatability and Scale

Process is the force that binds the other four forces of SPSCM together—**translating people's expertise, data's precision, and technology's potential into sustainable execution.** Well-defined and consistently applied processes create a foundation for scale, auditability, and continuous improvement.

Yet not all processes are visible, structured, or well-governed. Many are informal, ad hoc, or region-specific processes developed to compensate for gaps in tools or trust. These must be surfaced, understood, and either formalized or phased out to reduce risk and improve efficiency.

Processes – Unique to Each SPSCMs DNA

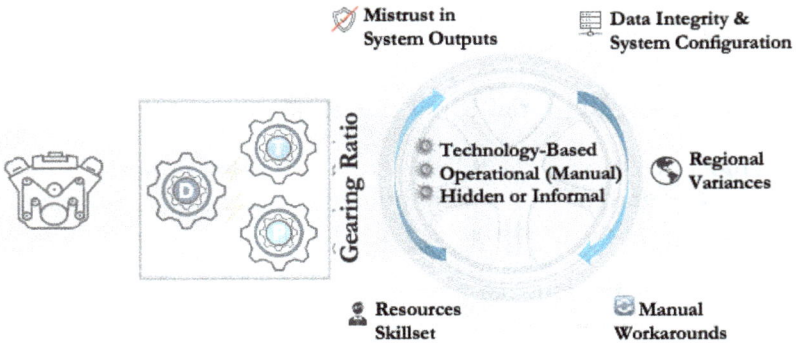

Mistrust in System Outputs

Data Integrity & System Configuration

Gearing Ratio

Technology-Based
Operational (Manual)
Hidden or Informal

Regional Variances

Resources Skillset

Manual Workarounds

Processes are driven by the unique mix of data, technology, and people. Efficiency and balance of business execution is governed by the characteristics of this ratio.

In the final chapter, we will bring the Five-Forces together, summarizing how **Data, Technology, People,** and **Process** interconnect to form a robust and adaptable SPSCM framework. The goal is not perfection in each force, but **alignment and balance**—ensuring that strengths in one area can compensate for gaps in another to drive sustainable performance in a long-lifecycle environment.

Closing Summary:
The Five-Forces Model of SPSCM Operations

SPSCM operates in a complex, high-variability environment where predictability is the exception, not the norm. Success in this space depends not on any single element, but on the **synchronized interplay of five foundational forces: Business Demands, Data, Technology, People,** and **Process.**

Each force represents a distinct dimension of the operation:

- **Business Demands** define what the supply chain must deliver—speed, reach, service levels, and cost targets shaped by product design, customer commitments, and global footprints.

- **Data** serves as the informational backbone, enabling forecasting, planning, and decision-making—if and only if it is clean, timely, and trusted.

- **Technology** acts as the execution platform, capable of accelerating and automating tasks but reliant on proper integration, configuration, and data quality.

- **People** provide judgment, adaptability, and critical thinking, especially in environments where no algorithm can fully account for real-world ambiguity.

- **Process** connects the moving parts, ensuring that all other forces operate with structure, clarity, and repeatability.

No two SPSCM organizations are configured the same. Differences in installed base, product complexity, customer expectations, regional policies, and available resources create a wide range of operating models. Some organizations lean heavily on people and process to compensate for limited technology. Others leverage advanced tools but struggle with data inconsistencies or a lack of internal expertise.

> **What matters most is not the strength of each individual force, but how well they are aligned to work together.**

Ultimately, the Five-Force model provides more than just a diagnostic framework—it also offers a roadmap for continuous improvement. Organizations must regularly assess the state of each force, identify misalignments or friction points, and recalibrate as conditions evolve. The goal is not equilibrium for its own sake, but **resilient performance** in the face of variability, disruption, and change.

In the next chapter, we shift from framework to application—laying the foundation for a **performance baseline** that will help organizations measure their current operational state, identify constraint points, and strategically adjust their "gearing ratios" across data, technology, and people. This baseline becomes the starting point for building a more efficient, adaptable, and high-performing SPSCM operation tailored to the unique demands of the business.

Chapter 17

Approach to Uncovering Inefficiencies in the SPSCM Five-Forces

When service parts supply chain management (SPSCM) leaders seek lasting operational improvements, they often launch initiatives under the banner of *transformation, optimization,* or *continuous improvement.* These initiatives typically revolve around performance targets—driven by profitability goals, customer expectations, or industry benchmarks—and are mapped into multi-year plans. Actions may include initiatives such as inventory reduction mandates, technology upgrades, outsourcing strategies, or network restructuring.

While well-intentioned, these efforts frequently overlook a critical question: **Will these changes truly lead to sustainable performance improvements—or will they simply shift the pressure elsewhere in the organization?** Too often, companies focus on visible symptoms without addressing the deeper operational forces that shape performance.

To drive effective and enduring change, organizations must go beyond surface-level problem-solving and develop a holistic understanding of the operational engine—specifically, the **Five-Forces** that govern SPSCM execution: **Business Demands, Data, Technology, People,** and **Process.**

From Strategy to Insight: Why the Five-Forces Matter

Every SPSCM operation has a unique "operational DNA" formed by how its Five-Forces interact. If one force is weak or misaligned, the others adapt—sometimes at the cost of efficiency, resilience, or customer satisfaction. For example, when data is unreliable, experienced personnel may compensate through intuition and manual workarounds. When technology lacks flexibility, processes bend to accommodate exceptions. These adaptations may preserve short-term continuity, but they also introduce risk, inconsistency, and hidden costs.

To uncover these dynamics, organizations must conduct deeper analysis and identify what truly drives their operational behavior. This begins with understanding the **undercurrents**—the informal, often invisible elements that shape day-to-day execution and constrain performance.

Most existing operational inefficiency resides under the surface

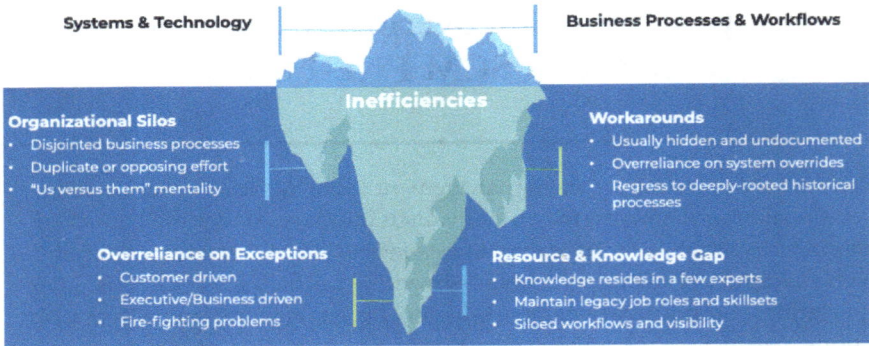

Systems & Technology | **Business Processes & Workflows**

Inefficiencies

Organizational Silos
- Disjointed business processes
- Duplicate or opposing effort
- "Us versus them" mentality

Workarounds
- Usually hidden and undocumented
- Overreliance on system overrides
- Regress to deeply-rooted historical processes

Overreliance on Exceptions
- Customer driven
- Executive/Business driven
- Fire-fighting problems

Resource & Knowledge Gap
- Knowledge resides in a few experts
- Maintain legacy job roles and skillsets
- Siloed workflows and visibility

Uncovering the Undercurrents of SPSCM

The Five-Forces framework provides a lens to assess not only what an SPSCM does, but HOW and WHY it operates the way it does. These undercurrents typically take the form of structural silos, reliance on workarounds, and institutional knowledge gaps.

1. Organizational Silos

Silos exist both **within** SPSCM and **between** SPSCM and other functional areas. Regional silos reflect differences in how data, systems, and processes have evolved over time. These silos often stem from historical decisions, regulatory constraints, or cultural differences that make standardization challenging. For example:

- Regional operations may run on legacy platforms while corporate headquarters uses newer systems.

- People and processes may diverge based on local interpretations of service levels or compliance needs.

Sales, field service, and product engineering frequently make decisions that ripple into SPSCM, without always recognizing the downstream consequences.

For instance:

- Aggressive SLAs promised by sales in remote markets may force SPSCM to overstock or incur high expedited shipping costs.

- Incomplete or outdated installed base data in CRM systems can derail proactive planning.

- Field service teams may overuse emergency requests or delay part returns, undermining inventory strategies.

Breaking down these silos requires more than organizational realignment—it also requires a shared understanding of how the Five-Forces interconnect across teams, regions, and roles.

2. Overreliance on Exceptions and Workarounds

SPSCM environments are highly reactive by nature—constantly managing urgent orders, customer escalations, supplier delays, and executive pressure. As a result, teams often default to manual interventions and local fixes when systems or processes fall short.

Common indicators of this dynamic include:

- Frequent overrides of system recommendations due to lack of trust in data or planning algorithms

- Unofficial processes developed by specific regions or individuals to bypass system limitations

- Lack of documentation for critical tasks, increasing dependence on tacit knowledge

While some workarounds are necessary, many persist due to unresolved root causes. Over time, these ad hoc fixes compound into systemic inefficiencies— creating a false sense of stability while masking deeper issues.

3. Resource and Knowledge Gaps

SPSCM expertise is rarely taught in formal education, which makes it heavily reliant on experiential learning. In organizations with high turnover or insufficient documentation, new employees may follow system outputs blindly—without the context to validate their accuracy.

Examples include:

- Mistaking high fill rates as indicators of good performance, despite customers experiencing delays

- Misinterpreting demand signals due to lack of understanding of service part behavior (e.g., infrequent but critical demand)

- Inability to differentiate between standard and exception-driven planning logic

Bridging these knowledge gaps requires a commitment to documentation, mentoring, and continuous learning—particularly around the implicit processes and exceptions that shape actual performance.

From Discovery to Action

By uncovering these undercurrents and evaluating the strength of each force, organizations gain clarity on what's really driving performance—and what's holding it back. This insight becomes the foundation for conducting a **Five-Forces Assessment**, a structured evaluation that measures the maturity, alignment, and constraints within each force across the organization.

In the next section, we will introduce this assessment approach and demonstrate how to interpret the results to guide targeted interventions.

Use Case: Diagnosing an Unexpected Fill Rate Drop

A global electronics OEM observed a sudden decline in its Asia-Pacific fill rates, despite high global inventory and stable system forecasts. Leadership initiated an investigation, expecting to find errors in planning algorithms or supplier performance.

However, a Five-Forces analysis revealed a more nuanced picture:

- **Data**: Installed base information in the CRM was outdated, underreporting service needs in rural regions
- **Technology**: Regional systems were not integrated with the central ERP, delaying stock visibility.
- **People**: Local planners had developed a workaround using spreadsheets, leading to unaligned order triggers.
- **Process**: The urgent order escalation process was poorly defined, causing misprioritization.
- **Business Demands**: A newly launched product had a contractual 24-hour SLA in remote locations—never communicated to global SPSCM leadership.

The root cause wasn't a single failure—it was a breakdown in alignment across the Five-Forces. By surfacing and addressing these hidden interdependencies, the company reestablished control. It updated its CRM, harmonized planning tools, and realigned regional teams.

Uncovering the Performance of the Five-Forces of SPSCM

The Five-Forces assessment approach in SPSCM is designed to uncover the real-world dynamics and constraints across a complex operational environment. It moves beyond theoretical frameworks and surface-level observations by investigating how **business demand, data, technologies, people**, and **processes** interact across the entire lifecycle of a service part—from inception to end-of-life.

This assessment is not just a diagnostic tool; it also forms the foundation for meaningful transformation. By examining how each force functions and interacts, companies can uncover systemic inefficiencies, root causes of underperformance, and risks hidden within their operations.

Conducting a Five-Forces Assessment – The Approach

Lifecycle-Centric Assessment

The assessment begins with tracking a **part's journey across its lifecycle**, spanning from initial design and engineering decisions to end-of-life decommissioning. This longitudinal approach reveals how decisions made in earlier phases impact downstream performance in forecasting, planning, field support, repair cycles, and reverse logistics. By mapping each lifecycle stage, the assessment identifies how forces influence different points in the chain and where the most frequent breakdowns or inefficiencies occur.

Multimodal Process Inclusion

Unlike traditional supply chain assessments, which often focus only on automated or digitized activities, this approach **intentionally includes manual, semi-automated, and fully automated processes**. This breadth is essential, as many field and legacy operations in SPSCM still rely heavily on email workflows, phone calls, spreadsheets, tacit knowledge, or partially integrated systems. These "off-system" or "gray zone" processes can be responsible for bottlenecks and delays, often hidden from system-level analytics.

By capturing **all modes of execution**—whether they reside in formal standard operating procedures (SOPs), ad hoc practices, or workaround processes—the assessment gains a fuller understanding of systemic capability and limitations.

Five-Forces Assessment – Process Mapping Example

Stage	Manual	Semi-Auto	Full-Auto	Forces Annotated	Validated
NPI	✓	✓		Data, Tech, People	✓
Forecasting	✓	✓		Data, Tech, People	✓
Procurement			✓	Tech, People	✓
Inventory Allocation		✓	✓	Process, Tech, People	
Returns	✓			Process, People	✓

Validation Checklist
✓ KPI Data Analysis
✓ Stakeholder Interviews
✓ System Audit Logs
✓ Exception Reports
✓ Root-Cause Analysis (Five-Whys)

Validation through KPI Evidence and Field Insights

To ensure that findings are grounded in reality, the assessment incorporates quantitative and qualitative validation techniques. This includes:

- **KPI-driven performance analysis**, such as fill rate, turnaround-time, first-time-fix-rate, parts availability, and excess/obsolete inventory metrics

- **Stakeholder interviews** and field-level observations that provide human insight into the reasons behind recurring issues, workarounds, or misalignments between system design and day-to-day reality

- **Exception logs, case studies, and root-cause analysis** (e.g., Five-Whys) to uncover persistent or systemic breakdowns not visible through dashboards alone.

Process Mapping and Diagnostic Approach

A structured process mapping methodology is essential for effectively assessing the Five-Forces in the SPSCM environment. Process mapping serves as the starting point, enabling visibility into how work actually flows across people, systems, locations, and technologies—not just how it's supposed to flow according to documentation.

This approach is particularly powerful in SPSCM, where process complexity is often buried in legacy workarounds, siloed knowledge, and hybrid execution models (manual/semi-automated/automated). Capturing the real state of operational execution provides the critical foundation for diagnosing performance issues, misalignments, and systemic risks across the Five-Forces.

Dual Diagnostic Tools: Five-Ways and the Expanded Five-Whys

The process mapping effort is structured around two complementary diagnostic approaches:

1. The Five-Ways of Process Enablement
2. The Five-Whys of Root Cause Analysis

The Five-Ways of Process Enablement Framework

The Five-Ways of Process Enablement is a diagnostic lens used to identify **how** a process is currently being executed in practice, across five key dimensions of the Five-Forces. Each force has an impact on how the process is performed.

Each "way" represents a layer of organizational behavior, system design, and performance dynamics that must be in sync for sustainable effectiveness. Each force has an impact on the others as part of the SPSCM ecosystem to execute the business. By establishing the Five-Ways of how each force is contributing to the operational execution today, will help to uncover the hidden inefficiencies or disconnects that need focus.

The Five-Ways include:

1. Way of Work (Process)

Each function within SPSCM is composed of numerous business processes that support execution routines. Identifying each process and analyzing how each force impacts them provides the assessment team with critical insights on where to focus attention.

- **Ideal State**: Documented, standardized, and continuously improved workflows optimized for agility and accuracy

- **In Practice**: Processes vary by region, often undocumented or heavily dependent on tacit knowledge or manual intervention.

- **Key Questions Include:**

  o Are planning and execution workflows clearly defined?

- o How is the task executed? (e.g., via SOP, work order, manual checklist, verbal instruction)
- o How frequently are SOPs reviewed and improved?
- o Are there hidden or undocumented steps?
- o Are the workflows aligned with system logic and user capabilities?
- o Is execution consistent across teams or regions?

- **SPSCM Examples:**

  - o Field service ticketing lacks integration with parts allocation.
  - o Failed parts reverse logistics vary by geography.

2. Way of System
Each process relies on one or more technology systems. Even fully manual processes often involve enabling technologies. These technologies must be identified and evaluated.

- **Ideal State:** Modular, scalable, and well-integrated systems tailored to support SPSCM-specific functions

- **In Practice:** Patchwork of legacy and modern systems, often maintained as disconnected silos

- **Key Questions Include:**

  - o What systems, platforms, or tools are used to support this process?
  - o Are systems integrated or standalone?
  - o Are users following system workflows, or bypassing them?

- **SPSCM Examples:**

  - o Inventory planning tool lacks real-time integration with ERP stock levels.
  - o Warehouse relies on legacy WMS that doesn't support serialized part tracking.

3. Way of Data
Similar to technology, data is foundational for process execution.

- **Ideal State:** Consistent, clean, and contextual data used across the value chain for proactive decision-making
- **In Practice:** Fragmented data pipelines, conflicting sources of truth, and manual reconciliation common

- **Key Questions Include:**

  - o What data is captured, ignored, manually entered, or duplicated?

- o Is there unified part master with lifecycle and substitution mapping?
- o Where are the critical data handoffs, and how reliable are they?
- o Is demand data reviewed and cleaned systematically?
- o Is data used for feedback or performance tuning?

- **SPSCM Examples:**

  - o SPBOM data used in repair depots doesn't match ERP configuration.
  - o MRO demand spikes not filtered from planning inputs, distorting forecasts.

4. Way of People

Processes vary in automation levels. However, human impact remains critical, even in automated processes, due to the need for checks and validation of outcomes.

- **Ideal State**: Skilled, aligned, and empowered teams that understand both the tools and the supply chain logic behind them

- **In Practice**: Adoption gaps, inconsistent training, and reliance on "super users" or individual heroics

- **Key Questions Include**:
  - o Who owns the process and who executes it?
  - o Are users trained in both the systems and the business logic?
  - o Are planners empowered to suggest system or process changes?
  - o Is there alignment between responsibility and authority?
  - o What skillsets, training, and support structures exist?

- **SPSCM Examples:**
  - o Planners bypass planning engines due to lack of trust in outputs.
  - o Regional teams maintain private Excel tools rather than using centralized platforms.

5. Way of Governance

Aligned with Business Demands, governance ensures the process outcomes meet expectations set by the business.

- **Ideal State**: Clear roles, escalation paths, data stewardship, and change control across all process and system layers

- **In Practice**: Governance is reactive, fragmented, and often seen as a compliance issue rather than an enabler.

- **Key Questions Include**:
  - Is there an operating model linking KPIs to decision-making forums?
  - Who owns system configurations and master data policies?
  - How are new processes and tech changes rolled out and enforced?
  - How is performance tracked, escalated, and improved?
  - Are there continuous improvement loops, or is the process static?

- **SPSCM Examples**:
  - No formal review process for demand planning accuracy
  - Conflicting inventory policies between global and regional governance bodies

The Five-Ways of SPSCM Process Enablement

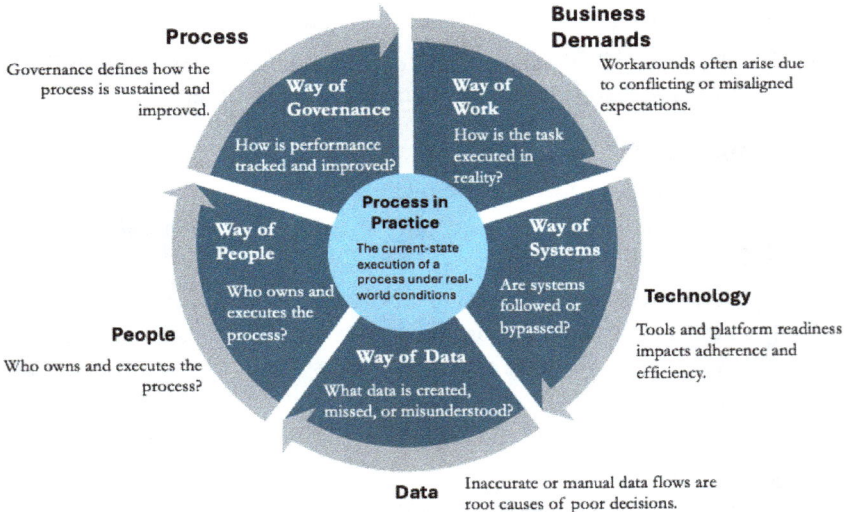

Process
Governance defines how the process is sustained and improved.

Business Demands
Workarounds often arise due to conflicting or misaligned expectations.

Way of Governance
How is performance tracked and improved?

Way of Work
How is the task executed in reality?

Process in Practice
The current-state execution of a process under real-world conditions

Way of People
Who owns and executes the process?

Way of Systems
Are systems followed or bypassed?

Technology
Tools and platform readiness impacts adherence and efficiency.

People
Who owns and executes the process?

Way of Data
What data is created, missed, or misunderstood?

Data
Inaccurate or manual data flows are root causes of poor decisions.

Using the Five-Ways approach helps the assessment team ask probing questions about how operations are actually performed. It also serves as a roadmap to identify processes that require deeper analysis using the Five-Whys technique, which is discussed next.

Visit this book's companion website at www.spscmfiveforces.com for expanded details on the Five-Ways approach as an effective diagnostics tool in process mapping.

The Five-Whys Root Cause Analysis

After Five-Ways mapping, the Five-Whys approach can be used to identify root causes of operational failures, exception handling, or performance erosion. Originally developed for engineering and quality control, this method is ideal to use throughout the process mapping phase in SPSCM.

The Five-Whys analysis helps uncover the true root cause of underperformance. Rather than settling for surface-level reasons (e.g., "the system didn't update"), analysts probe iteratively.

Examples of initial "why" questions include:

- **Why** was the part not available?

- **Why** was it not ordered on time?

- **Why** did the planning engine miss the demand signal?

- **Why** was the usage data incomplete?

- **Why** wasn't the local technician trained to escalate?

This line of inquiry reveals weaknesses across data quality, system logic, field practices, and organizational behavior—all connected to the Five-Forces. It also distinguishes between symptomatic and systematic problems.

Five Whys Example: Stocking Level Overrides

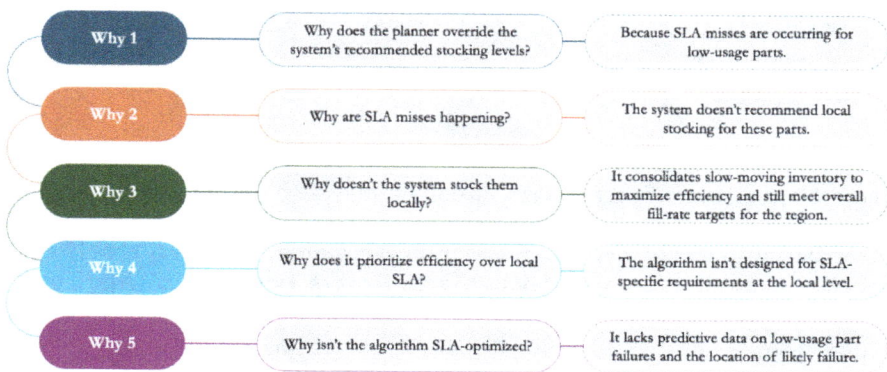

Why 1	Why does the planner override the system's recommended stocking levels?	Because SLA misses are occurring for low-usage parts.
Why 2	Why are SLA misses happening?	The system doesn't recommend local stocking for these parts.
Why 3	Why doesn't the system stock them locally?	It consolidates slow-moving inventory to maximize efficiency and still meet overall fill-rate targets for the region.
Why 4	Why does it prioritize efficiency over local SLA?	The algorithm isn't designed for SLA-specific requirements at the local level.
Why 5	Why isn't the algorithm SLA-optimized?	It lacks predictive data on low-usage part failures and the location of likely failure.

Root-Cause: Inadequate predictive data leads to system limitations, requiring manual planner intervention.

Five-Forces Framing:

- **Process**: Manual override is necessary due to SLA risk.
- **Technology**: Algorithm favors efficiency over service.
- **People**: Planners mitigate risks manually.
- **Data**: It's missing predictive failure indicators.
- **Business Demand**: Aggressive SLAs demand high availability.

Extend Process Assessment to the Root-Reason - Example

With the first level of "whys" and root-cause identified, the next layer of extended Five-Whys can be applied.

Returning to the example of the stocking level override process:

Root Cause Identified: A lack of predictive data on low-usage failures.

Applying the Five-Whys again:

Expanded Five Whys Example: Low-Usage Part Data Availability

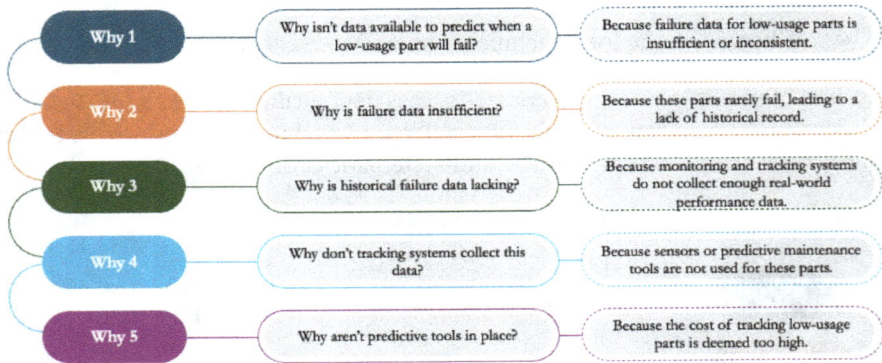

Why 1	Why isn't data available to predict when a low-usage part will fail?	Because failure data for low-usage parts is insufficient or inconsistent.
Why 2	Why is failure data insufficient?	Because these parts rarely fail, leading to a lack of historical record.
Why 3	Why is historical failure data lacking?	Because monitoring and tracking systems do not collect enough real-world performance data.
Why 4	Why don't tracking systems collect this data?	Because sensors or predictive maintenance tools are not used for these parts.
Why 5	Why aren't predictive tools in place?	Because the cost of tracking low-usage parts is deemed too high.

Root-Reason Identified: The lack of investment in predictive tools prevents accurate forecasting of part failures, sustaining the need for manual overrides.

By establishing clear process maps and using structured techniques like the Five-Whys, organizations gain a **360-degree view of execution reality**. The analysis reveals not only where processes break down, but how and why they diverge from design—highlighting the forces influencing that divergence.

Why These Methods Matter in SPSCM Contexts

These methods are especially powerful in environments where:

- **High-cost, low-velocity parts** require tailored sourcing and repair models.
- **Field service and depot repair processes** are decentralized and operate under different local norms.
- **Legacy systems** support mission-critical work but lack modern integration or real-time visibility.
- **Demand variability and exception handling** are the rule, not the exception.

Mapping these real-world conditions helps uncover how failure loops form—for example, how a technician's decision to hoard a critical part may stem from repeated stock-outs, which, in turn, stem from upstream planning errors due to poor data quality or misaligned KPIs.

Bridging from Process Mapping to Data, Technology, and People Assessment

As Five-Ways and Five-Whys analysis unfolds, a pattern becomes clear: many of the process breakdowns and force-driven friction points do not originate solely from poor process design or operational shortcuts. Instead, they often trace back to deeper, structural limitations embedded in three foundational enablers of the service parts supply chain—**data, technology,** and **people**.

Examples:

- A recurring stockout at a regional field depot may initially appear to be a demand planning failure. However, Five-Whys analysis may reveal the root cause lies in **incomplete or misaligned asset install base data,** which in turn undermines forecasting accuracy.
- A delayed repair cycle time might seem like a technician scheduling issue, but further probing may uncover an outdated legacy system lacking integration with real-time parts availability.
- Escalation paths may stall, not because of poor process logic, but because **roles and responsibilities are unclear or fragmented** across organizational boundaries, leaving frontline workers to rely on tacit knowledge rather than structured authority.

These examples illustrate a critical pivot in the Five-Forces assessment: once operational processes have been clearly mapped and their failure points examined, **the true sources of risk and underperformance typically lead upstream**—into how data is structured and governed, how technology enables or constrains execution, and how people are aligned, trained, and empowered.

From Process to Root-Cause: A Deeper Lens

Process mapping provides the "what" and "how" of execution, examining the data, technology, and people layers answers the "why it fails" and "why it varies" questions at scale. These elements are not standalone silos—they are force multipliers. Each has the power to reinforce or erode process discipline, customer experience, and service outcomes depending on how well they are designed, connected, and maintained.

Root-Cause Diagnostic Frameworks for Data, Technology, and People

To expand a bit deeper into the Data, Technology and People Forces during the assessment process, it is essential to establish a comprehensive and detailed understanding of what is driving the previously identified root causes.

1. Data Assessment Framework: From Noise to Signal

When data issues emerge as root causes—such as inconsistent planning inputs, asset location mismatches, or incorrect failure codes—organizations must perform a structured data assessment. The following framework helps break this down:

a. Data Quality Dimensions:
Use standard data quality metrics to evaluate the datasets underpinning key SPSCM processes:

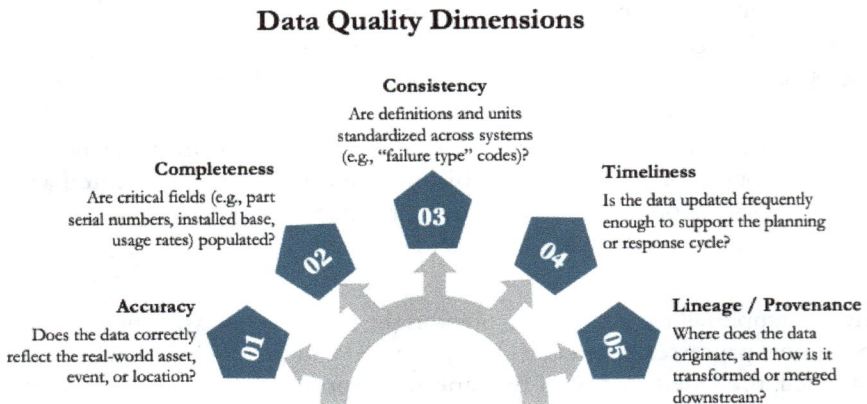

Data Quality Dimensions

Consistency
Are definitions and units standardized across systems (e.g., "failure type" codes)?

Completeness
Are critical fields (e.g., part serial numbers, installed base, usage rates) populated?

Timeliness
Is the data updated frequently enough to support the planning or response cycle?

Accuracy
Does the data correctly reflect the real-world asset, event, or location?

Lineage / Provenance
Where does the data originate, and how is it transformed or merged downstream?

01 02 03 04 05

b. Critical Data Object Mapping:
Map the most influential data objects across the SPSCM lifecycle—e.g., Part Master, Service BOM, Install Base, Asset History, Technician Logs—and trace how and where they are used in forecasting, fulfillment, triage, or reverse logistics.

c. Stakeholder Interviews & Data Pain-Points Matrix:
Conduct structured interviews with data consumers and data stewards to surface use-case-specific gaps. Create a matrix that links data fields to failure modes or process delays observed in earlier process mapping.

2. Technology Assessment Framework: Fit-for-Purpose & Interoperability

Technology is a frequent root cause in SPSCM due to patchwork systems, legacy tools, and limited integration. A strong assessment should cover:

a. Technology Maturity Mapping:
Score key systems across domains—ERP, WMS, Field Service, Predictive Analytics, and Diagnostic Tools—against a maturity model:

- **Manual** (spreadsheet, email-driven)

- **Basic Digital** (transactional systems with silos)

- **Integrated** (API-connected, real-time visibility)

- **Predictive** (ML forecasting, prescriptive recommendations)

- **Autonomous** (self-healing or auto-replenishment workflows)

b. System Interoperability Heatmap:
Visualize how well core systems exchange data across the SPSCM ecosystem. Highlight pain points such as:

- Duplicate entry/manual syncs

- Batch file dependencies

- Lack of real-time integration

- ERP-to-WMS or ERP-to-FS gaps

c. Use-Case Based Stress Testing:
Select real service use cases—e.g., part ordering after diagnostic, triage escalations, depot replenishment—and simulate system interactions to identify latency, friction, or error propagation across platforms.

3. People & Organizational Assessment: Skills, Roles, and Alignment

Service parts supply chains are only as strong as the people who interpret diagnostic data, initiate repairs, coordinate replenishment, or escalate supplier issues. Root-cause assessments here should include:

a. Role Clarity and Accountability Mapping:
Use a **RACI model** to assess who is RESPONSIBLE, ACCOUNTABLE, CONSULTED, and INFORMED at each major process step (e.g., triage, order fulfillment, reverse logistics). Common gaps include duplicated responsibility or unassigned escalation triggers.

b. Capability and Skills Inventory:
Survey or interview functional teams (planning, repair, customer support, depot operations) using a skills matrix across technical (system usage, data analysis), functional (S&OP, demand planning), and soft skills (collaboration, escalation).

c. Culture and Decision Autonomy Diagnostics:
Assess cultural barriers to performance—e.g., do technicians feel empowered to override planned orders based on field realities? Are depot managers rewarded for short-term cost cutting or long-term uptime? Include behavioral interviews to uncover systemic blockers or misaligned incentives.

Tying It Together: The Cross-Domain Root-Cause Tree

To close the loop, document the findings from these assessments in a unified **root-cause tree** or **dashboard** that links:

- → **Observed failure (process map)**
- → **Immediate breakdown point**
- → **Root cause in data, tech, or people**
- → **Force(s) from Five-Forces it aligns with (e.g., Supplier Risk, Customer Expectation, Complexity, Internal Friction, Regulation)**

This integrated view is essential for prioritizing which foundational elements to transform first, and for aligning stakeholders across functions around common causes and shared goals.

Chapter Summary:
Conducting a Five-Forces Assessment
in Service Parts Supply Chain Management (SPSCM)

This chapter presented a practical methodology for applying the Five-Forces framework to assess operational and strategic performance within SPSCM. By tracking a part's lifecycle from inception to end-of-life, the assessment reveals how systemic pressures—such as supplier risk, customer expectations, internal friction, complexity, and regulation—manifest in day-to-day failures, delays, and inefficiencies.

The assessment begins with detailed **process mapping**, anchored in tools like the **Five-Ways** and **Expanded Five-Whys** framework to uncover failure points. From there, the root causes are categorized across **data, technology, and people** domains. This structured approach creates a diagnostic thread from observable process issues all the way to underlying systemic forces.

To support practitioners, the chapter introduced several practical tools:

- A **Process Mapping Framework** that tracks tasks from manual to automated stages
- A **Critical Data Object Mapping** that outlines key data entities and lifecycle touchpoints
- A **Stakeholder Interview & Data Pain-Point Matrix** that links user feedback to specific data gaps and process delays
- A **System Interoperability Heatmap** to visualize where data exchange breaks down among ERP, WMS, CRM, and other systems.
- A **Cross-Domain Root-Cause Tree**, which ties operational failures back to specific root causes and their alignment with one or more of the Five-Forces.

Together, these tools enable a comprehensive view of how operational breakdowns link to strategic vulnerabilities, and where targeted improvements can drive both near-term efficiency and long-term resilience.

Template Downloads
Additional details of the Five-Forces Assessment discussed in this chapter are available for free download from the companion website
www.spscmfiveforces.com.

Final Thoughts

Service Parts Supply Chain Management (SPSCM) operates fundamentally differently from the traditional forward supply chain. While both share similar customer-facing paths and nomenclature, their underlying business models and execution diverge significantly. The forward supply chain is designed to produce known products with a defined bill of materials, each directly tied to production. In contrast, SPSCM functions within a highly complex "just-in-case" speculative framework, where required service parts are known, but failure timelines depend on numerous unpredictable variables—many outside SPSCM's control.

This inherent uncertainty, coupled with stringent customer Service Level Agreements (SLAs), necessitates strategic inventory staging across multi-echelon networks. SPSCM must strike a delicate balance between ensuring part availability and managing inventory lifecycle challenges, often spanning years or even decades. This extended lifecycle often exacerbates forecasting errors, leading to excess inventory, obsolescence, and high scrapping rates. Each service part's lifecycle stage requires distinct management strategies, further adding to the complexity of an already intricate operation.

Benchmarking and Challenges

SPSCM is arguably one of the most complex functions within a company, requiring skilled professionals who thrive in an environment where daily tasks are both demanding and dynamic. However, no two SPSCMs are alike, even within the same industry. Differences in company culture, product portfolios, technology stacks, data processing capabilities, and inventory networks create vastly different performance metrics.

Additionally, SPSCM's reliance on cross-functional data and decision-making makes standard benchmarking particularly difficult. Traditional performance comparisons often fail to capture the unique constraints and challenges each SPSCM organization faces, limiting the effectiveness of external benchmarking efforts. Instead, organizations must adopt customized measurement frameworks tailored to their unique operating conditions.

Path to Lasting Change

For organizations seeking to optimize, transform, or innovate their SPSCM, success begins with first understanding why current processes exist and how they operate within the Five-Forces of SPSCM. Comprehensive audits are essential to uncover inefficiencies caused by inadequate solutions, underperforming technology, poor data quality, or systems incapable of managing complexity.

More importantly, assessing the Five-Forces—business demand, data, technology, people, and process—establishes a baseline for how the SPSCM operates and why it functions as it does. This baseline serves as a foundation for targeted improvements that align with business objectives.

With a clear strategy, thorough audits, and a tailored roadmap, organizations can progressively refine SPSCM into a more resilient and efficient operation. Despite the inherent constraints of the "just-in-case" model, meaningful improvements are achievable. By strengthening data, technology, people, and processes, companies can enhance agility, predictability, and efficiency— ensuring SPSCM delivers maximum value within the parameters set by business demand and their unique Five-Forces footprint.

For additional information visit the book's companion website at:
www.spscmfiveforces.com

The Five-Forces of SPSCM Operations

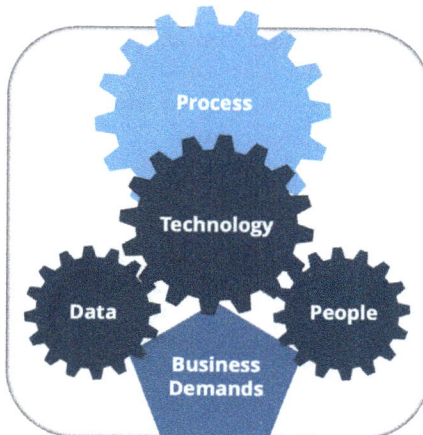

ABOUT THE AUTHOR

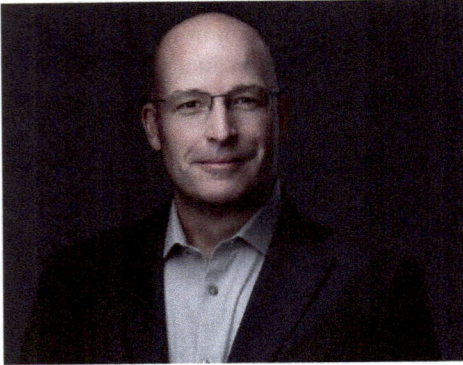

Mark Brenzikofer is a seasoned field service and service supply chain professional with thirty years of operational, executive, and solution design expertise. He has worked with large, diverse, and global companies across industries and regions.

A decade into his career, Mark transitioned from field service engineering to service parts supply chain management, driven by a mission to address and resolve the service parts issues that plagued field service organizations. As he delved deeper into the challenges, complexities, and demands of Service Parts Supply Chain Management (SPSCM), he realized there was no simple solution.

Over the past two decades, Mark has collaborated with companies across North America, South America, Europe, and Asia, helping assess the strengths and weaknesses of their SPSCM operations. His tailored frameworks and solutions have enhanced service supply chain performance globally. Through discovery sessions, day-in-the-life interviews, and data-driven analysis, he engages closely with clients to uncover improvement opportunities aligned with business goals.

Mark holds an Executive MBA in International Business from the University of Texas at Dallas, and a B.S. in Electronic Engineering Technology from DeVry University in Kansas City, Missouri. He is also certified by the Association of Supply Chain Management (ASCM/APICS) with a Certificate in Transformation for Supply Chain (CTSC).

Mark currently resides in Dallas, Texas, USA.

Email: Markb@profoundtransformations.com

Glossary

Supply Chain Disciplines

- **FSC** – *Forward Supply Chain*: The operational process of procuring raw material, manufacturing a product, and delivering it to an end customer or sales channel.
- **FSCM** – *Forward Supply Chain Management*: The management process, control, and oversight of the forward supply chain.
- **SPSC** – *Service Parts Supply Chain*: A specialized discipline within supply chain focused on delivering service parts for product repair and maintenance.
- **SPSCM** – *Service Parts Supply Chain Management*: The management, control, and oversight of the service parts supply chain.

Industry and Operations

- **FS** – *Field Service*: The delivery of repair and maintenance work at a customer site.
- **JIT** – *Just-in-Time*: A production system utilized in the forward supply chain where materials and parts are received or manufactured only when they are needed to meet immediate customer demand.
- **MRO** – *Maintenance, Repair, and Operations*: A type of service parts supply chain performing essential activities needed to keep a manufacturing facility—including production equipment—in working order.
- **OEM** – *Original Equipment Manufacturer*: The company that designs and builds products that are sold to another firm.
- **PM** – *Preventive Maintenance*: Scheduled service to avoid breakdown.
- **POS** – *Point-of-Sale*: The location or system where sales transactions occur, often used in demand signal capture.
- **SLA** – *Service Level Agreement*: A contract or performance benchmark between a service provider and a client.
- **SOP** – *Service-Only Provider*: A third-party service vendor that performs repairs or maintenance but does not manufacture products.
- **WIP** – *Work-in-Progress*: Goods that are in production but not yet completed.

Technology and Systems

- **AI** – *Artificial Intelligence*: Machine learning and cognitive systems used to simulate human decision-making.

- **API** – *Application Programming Interface*: A set of rules that allow different software systems to communicate.
- **IT** – *Information Technology*: System and tools that support data processing and connectivity.
- **ML** – *Machine Learning*: A subset of AI focused on data-driven algorithm learning.

Engineering and Configuration

- **BOM** – *Bill of Materials*: A list of components needed to manufacture or repair a product.
- **GPS** – *Global Positioning System*: Location-tracking tool used in field service or logistics.
- **HVAC** – *Heating, Ventilation, and Air Conditioning*: A key system in building management and a common service part domain.
- **MBOM** – *Manufacturing Bill of Materials*: Bill of materials tailored to the components required for manufacturing a product.
- **SPBOM** – *Service Parts Bill of Materials*: Bill of materials tailored to the components required for service and repair.

Planning and Execution

- **EOL** – *End-of-Life*: The point when a product is no longer supported or produced.
- **FRU** – *Field Replaceable Unit*: A service part that can be replaced during a repair or maintenance event.
- **LTB** – *Last-Time-Buy*: Final opportunity to purchase a part before it becomes obsolete.
- **MEIO** – *Multi-Echelon Inventory Optimization*: Technique for managing inventory across multiple tiers of the service parts supply chain.
- **NBD** – *Next Business Day*: A common commitment window in service parts SLAs.
- **PLC** – *Product Life Cycle*: The stages a product goes through from development to retirement.
- **S&OP** – *Sales and Operations Planning*: A process to align production, inventory, forecast, and demand in the forward supply chain.
- **SKU** – *Stock Keeping Unit*: A unique identifier for each distinct product or service item.

Platforms and Tools

- **CRM** – *Customer Relationship Management*: Systems to manage customer interactions and data.
- **ERP** – *Enterprise Resource Planning*: Integrated systems managing business processes and data across functions.
- **MRP** – *Materials Requirements Planning*: A planning tool for scheduling and inventory control.
- **SAP** – *Systems Applications and Products*: A leading ERP platform used for enterprise-wide process management.
- **TMS** – *Transportation Management System*: Software for planning and executing freight movement.
- **WMS** – *Warehouse Management System*: Tools for managing inventory within a warehouse.

Distribution Centers

- **CSR** – *Country Stock Room*: Inventory stockroom within the multi-echelon network located within a country.
- **CDC** – *Central Distribution Center*: Core hub in the multi-echelon network managing inbound/outbound inventory for broader areas.
- **GDC** – *Global Distribution Center*: International hub servicing cross-border demand.
- **LSR** – *Local Stock Room*: On-site or near-site parts depot within the multi-echelon network, often at field service locations.
- **RDC** – *Regional Distribution Center*: Inventory hubs within the multi-echelon network located within major geographic regions.

Process and Governance

- **RACI** – *Responsible, Accountable, Consulted, Informed*: A governance model for defining ownership, roles, and responsibilities for a process.
- **SOP** – *Standard Operating Procedure*: Documented guidelines for how to execute tasks consistently.

Compliance, Tax, and Responsibility

- **VAT** – *Value Added Tax*: Consumption tax that is levied on the "value added" at each stage of the production and distribution chain of goods and services.
- **WEEE** – *Waste Electrical and Electronic Equipment*: European Union (EU) directive for recycling electronics.

Maintenance Metrics

- **KPI** – *Key-Performance Indicator*: Metrics used to measure success and performance of supply chain operations.
- **MTBF** – *Mean-Time-Between-Failure*: A reliability metric that tracks uptime between product breakdowns.
- **MTBPM** – *Mean-Time-Between-Preventative-Maintenance*: Average interval between preventive service action.
- **MTTR** – *Mean-Time-to-Repair*: Average time required to complete a repair, including waiting on service parts delivery.
- **TAT** – *Turnaround Time*: The time from receiving a part until it's returned to service or ready for shipment.